WEEKEND
WOODTURNING
PROJECTS

WEEKEND WOODTURNING PROJECTS

25 SIMPLE PROJECTS FOR THE HOME

MARK BAKER

The Taunton Press

The Taunton Press
Inspiration for hands-on living®

The Taunton Press, Inc., 63 South Main Street
P.O. Box 5506, Newtown, CT 06470-5506
e-mail: tp@taunton.com

First published 2014 by
Guild of Master Craftsman Publications Ltd.
Castle Place, 166 High Street, Lewes, East Sussex BN7 1XU

Library of Congress Cataloging-in-Publication Data in progress

Publisher: Jonathan Bailey
Production Manager: Jim Bulley
Managing Editor: Gerrie Purcell
Senior Project Editor: Wendy McAngus
Editor: Richard Webb
Managing Art Editor: Gilda Pacitti
Designer: Simon Goggin
Photographer: Anthony Bailey
Technical drawings: Mark Carr
Photograph of Jet 1221VS lathe (505073) on page 10
courtesy of Axminster Tool Centre Ltd.

Color origination by GMC Reprographics
Printed and bound in China

CONTENTS

PROJECTS

INTRODUCTION

Turning is a rich and wonderful woodworking discipline. I was fortunate to have the support of turners who were willing to spend time and a not inconsiderable amount of effort teaching me how to turn. They introduced me to the lathe, showed me how to use the tools, and taught me the skills I'd need to actually make things. Their patient guidance and support meant that I was never overwhelmed, and I always felt there was someone there to explain and help when things didn't go according to plan.

The first time I made something on my own on the lathe I was hooked. The projects I was given to make started with spindle turning – turning between centers. All my mentors claimed (and I cannot in hindsight disagree with them) that spindle turning will develop fine tool control and the ability to see how shapes work together more quickly than faceplate turning.

So the projects started with spindle turning. Only when my tutors thought my tool control was good enough did they let me venture into faceplate turning. I realized that each project they gave me was a skill-building exercise, with each task getting just a little bit harder while still being fun to make. It was never boring, and after many years I still love being at the lathe.

The book is intended to appeal to turners who are looking for projects that will help them develop their skills. I have included 25 projects that gradually build your skills and demonstrate the key turning processes and techniques. The projects included are similar to the ones I first tackled, and they have stood me in great stead since. I will show the key stages for making each project, giving advice, hints, tips, and reminders along the way to help you throughout. For the purpose of this book, I have assumed that the reader will be someone who is relatively new to turning, but has a mini-lathe with a 12-in. (300mm) swing, a basic turning tool selection, a chuck, mounting accessories, and some common workshop equipment, and knows the fundamentals of using this equipment.

My mentors said it was no use turning if you didn't have fun. Yes, I have days when things do not go according to plan, but I always enjoy it. I hope you like the book and have fun in your turning ventures.

Mark Baker

TOOLS, EQUIPMENT AND SAFETY

TOOLS AND EQUIPMENT

LATHES

Lathes come in all shapes and sizes to suit all workshop areas and sizes of projects. For the purposes of this book I have designed all the projects to be created on a lathe with a 12-in. (300mm) swing (the largest diameter workpiece it can handle) and a minimum of 15 in. (350mm) between centers. Of course you can use a bigger lathe, but they are invariably more expensive. Whether you use a variable speed lathe or one with a drive belt on stepped pulleys is up to you. I would say that the variable speed ones, although costing more, do make things a little easier and give you more options in terms of speed. A few rpm up or down sometimes help to minimize vibration.

Whatever you use, make sure it is supported by a good bench or stand and that it is securely attached to it. The heavier and more sturdy the stand or bench, the better its vibration-dampening qualities.

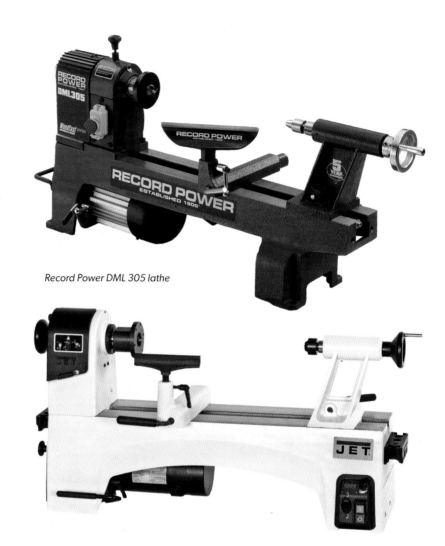

Record Power DML 305 lathe

Jet 1221VS lathe

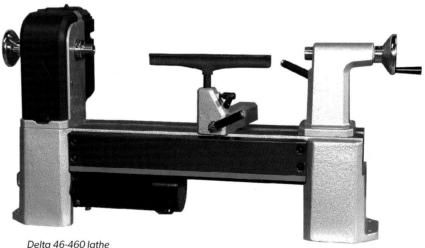

Delta 46-460 lathe

CHUCKS, DRIVES, AND CENTERS

I have made the assumption people will use a scroll chuck. Most turners now use them, and they do make life easier. There are numerous chucks and work-mounting accessories for turners. The projects in this book require a basic scroll chuck – 4 in. (100mm) or close to this will be ideal – a set of dovetail- or gripper-type jaws that can lock down onto a tenon no more than 2⅝ in. (70mm) in diameter. A little more capacity than this would be helpful but not essential.

The key with tenons is to have as large a size as possible to increase stability without compromising your ability to shape the work. Too small a tenon in relation to the size of the work means the piece will not be supported properly while it is being cut, increasing the risk of breaking the tenon, especially on faceplate-orientated grain.

Some of the projects in this book use a screw chuck that fits directly onto the headstock spindle or one that is mounted in the chuck jaws. Chucks are often supplied with a screw chuck as standard equipment or as an optional accessory. If you do not have one, you can use a faceplate instead.

Like chucks, drives and centers come in all shapes and sizes. For these projects, a standard two- or four-prong drive will suffice, along with a standard point center. I typically use a combination of a point and ring center. The ring center is the one I use the most because it spreads the bearing load over a bigger area. It also allows me to more easily reverse the work so I can finish the base, and it minimizes the risk of splitting the small stub of wood remaining. We will look at that later. An alternative is to use a standard point center, put a bit of adhesive putty on the point, and place a washer on the putty so that only ⅛ in. (3mm) of the point sticks out. When this is placed into the wood, the washer spreads the load and does almost the same job as the ring center.

Scroll chucks, faceplates, and screw chucks

Drives and centers

TOOLS USED

Tools are vital to enable you to shape the work, but there are so many that it can become confusing. I have used very few turning tools for these projects. I use a basic set of turning tools, shown in the photo below. The sizes I use are ideal for starting out, and you can alter the mix later on as you progress. For instance, if you go for a bigger lathe, you may find you need to have some bigger gouges.

I mention two parting tools: a beading and parting tool and a thinner one. I like using two purely because I can use the larger tool when rolling large beads and cutting tenons. But when cutting off waste or working on smaller work, such as a box joint, I may not want to remove so much, so I prefer having a thin parting tool for this. There are many to choose from, ranging from about 1/16 in. (1.5mm) upward. The top photo on the facing page

shows a few different sorts in varying sizes. If you only have one, I would suggest you opt for the 1/4 in. (6mm).

I also use scrapers. These are used to refine a surface after you have done the shaping with a gouge. There are a couple of routes you can take. One is to go for conventional rectangular scrapers with shaped ends – a French curve for internal curves, and either a square across or angled cutting edge for external curves. You can introduce a third type of end if you choose, which has a shallow curvature on the front for cutting shallow internal curves.

The second route, and probably the cheaper and more flexible of the two, is to opt for a multi-tipped tool. There are many types and makes available. These are effectively a handled bar that accepts a variety of tips.

Either round, square, or shaped bar versions can be found. Most come as a package with a selection of tips, and often they have a facility to swivel the tip or an articulated head arrangement to alter the tip position (bottom photo on the facing page). There are large tips for refining work like conventional scrapers and smaller tips that help with hollowing out work, particularly endgrain or deeper work.

These are tools to refine or shape work. If you use a round bar version, the tip can be presented in standard scraping mode or rotated to present the cutter in shear scraping mode for a finer cut. I use both of these tools in the projects, but you need only one, as either will meet all the requirements presented in the following 25 projects.

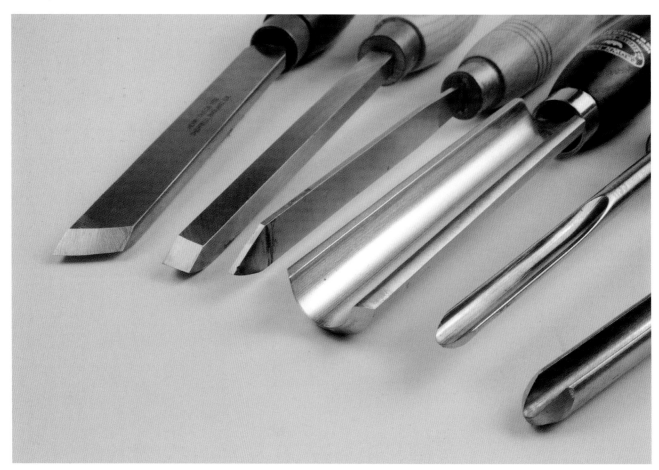

From left to right: ¾-in. (19mm) skew chisel, ⅜-in. (10mm) beading and parting tool, ⅛-in. (3mm) parting tool, ¾-in. (19mm) spindle roughing gouge, ⅜-in. (10mm) spindle gouge, and ⅜-in. (10mm) bowl gouge.

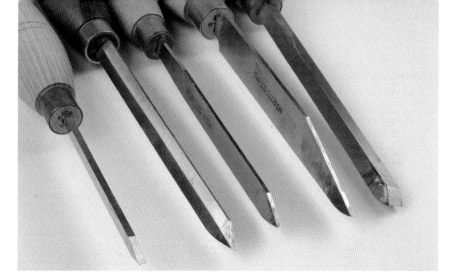

Various sizes of parting tools

OPTIONAL EXTRA

I have introduced one extra tool that can be considered an optional extra and is one I use in some projects. It is a small ⅛-in. (3mm) bead-forming tool. Smaller beads may be tricky to cut with conventional tools, especially if located in hard-to-reach areas. When multiple identical small beads are required, this is my go-to tool. But of course, it is a luxury and you can get by with other tools, although multiple small beads do require good tool control to get right. Many manufacturers supply bead-cutting tools. The one pictured below is used flute down on the rest and the cutting edge is gently pushed into the wood until you get to the required bead form. Do not use it to reduce the diameter of the work; only use the tool on the surface of the wood. The crown of the bead should be the tip of the surface being worked.

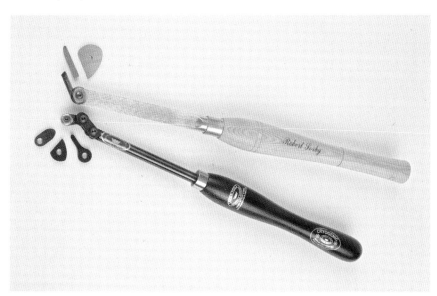

Selection of scrapers

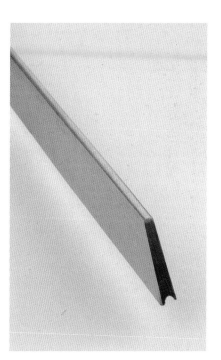

Bead-forming tool

Multi-tipped tools

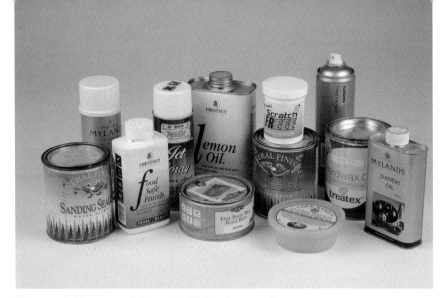

Numerous finishes are available worldwide to suit your preferences.

FINISHING

There are whole books written about finishes. My favorite finish is a Danish oil. Although I do use an aerosol spray lacquer for one of the projects, for the others I use either oil or a paste wax. I have tried to keep things simple. Oil finishes are durable, easy to apply, and can be obtained in either matte, satin, or gloss luster. Some of the pieces featured in this book may come into contact with food, so where this is the case, make sure that the finish you have chosen is safe for the purpose. Many will say so on the packaging. I use paper towel or a brush to apply the oil or wax to the work, followed by paper towel to remove the excess later. As with anything, I recommend experimenting with different finishes to find out what you like. There is so much fun to be had doing this and you will find that different finishes can change the look of the work quite dramatically.

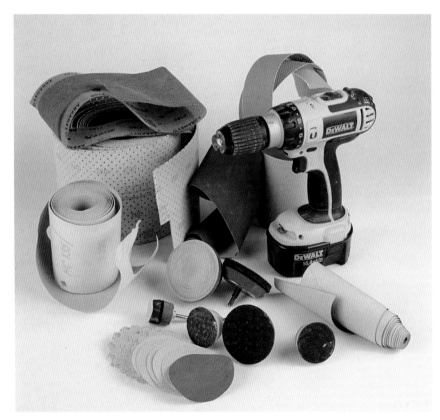

A drill, various grades of abrasive, and power sanding arbors help no end.

ABRASIVES

After shaping your work, you will need to sand it to a fine finish. There are numerous grit grades and types of abrasive to choose from. I would recommend aluminum oxide to start with; it is up to you whether you use it by hand or use hook-and-loop-backed abrasive attached to a sanding arbor held in a drill. I use both hand and power sanding methods. You should not power sand right up against detail, such as beads or coves; these areas should only be sanded by hand. If power sanding, a 2- or 3-in. (50 or 75mm) arbor is all you need for these projects. Of course, if you power sand you need a drill. You also need one when drilling a hole for a screw chuck, but most people have one in the workshop.

The projects require nothing finer than 400-grit abrasive. I have used 120, 180, 240, 320, and 400-grit abrasives. Of course, use coarser or finer if you need. Whatever grit grade you start with, it should be coarse enough to remove any damage or surface deviation. The subsequent grit grades just remove the scratches left from the previous one until you cannot see them any more. Always work through the grits and never skip any.

One piece of equipment that I find handy when working on vases and hollow forms is a pair of forceps. They are handy for holding abrasives and cloth when sanding or finishing in hard-to-reach places. One word of warning: never hold them by the handle holes, only hold the shaft. If you ever get a catch with them, you do not want your fingers trapped in the holes.

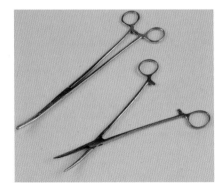

Forceps help with sanding deep or hard-to-reach areas.

ADDITIONAL WORKSHOP GEAR

There are a few more pieces of equipment used in this book that, although often overlooked, are nonetheless useful. Some have to do with measuring and marking. A rule, a tape measure, and calipers of some sort are helpful when turning, as we all need to know sizes and gauge things for fit.

I use a reverse turning method on some work, which necessitates the removal of a small stub of wood to finish off the work after I have refined and shaped the base or foot area. I use a chisel for this – either a carving chisel or a woodworking chisel is fine. I also use a saw to remove sections of wood or the work from waste wood after shaping. This is done with the lathe off; that is safer than parting off the piece with the lathe running. You do not need anything mighty; a small fine-toothed saw will work nicely.

I use a screw chuck for some work, which requires a drill and a suitable drill bit, and a drill chuck with a Morse taper to fit the tailstock of the lathe. The chuck holds various drill bits. These chucks can help when removing waste in some turnings, such as a hollow form or vase. One project, the salt or pepper mill, has an internal hollow that needs to be precisely dimensioned to fit the mill mechanism used. This is more easily done by using drill bits held in the drill chuck.

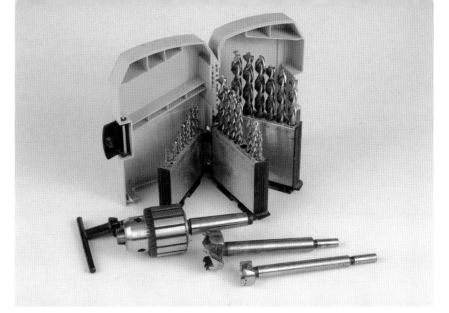

A drill chuck with a selection of brad-point bits and a few Forstner bits will help with your work.

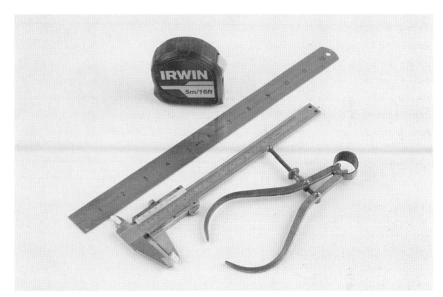

A variety of measuring tools is helpful.

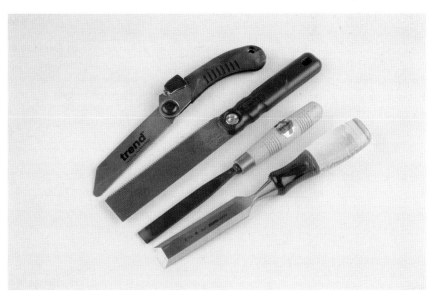

A saw and a carving or bench chisel are helpful.

WOOD

I have not gone down the prescriptive "what woods to use" route. That's because the availability of various types of wood differs wildly from area to area and country to country. I have, however, made recommendations. Whether you choose to use local woods, sustainable woods, or woods from far-flung locations is up to you. There are many wonderful species available; the choices are myriad and endlessly fascinating. With one exception, I have chosen to limit mine to local woods that are easily turned. I would advise you to explore woods that can be worked easily and those that hold detail well – typically close-grained hardwoods. As your skills develop you can move onto more expensive woods and try out a wider variety to experience for yourself their differences and learn first-hand how to deal with open grain, burls, and so on.

The projects are a mixture of woods, some small offcuts (one from plywood from the workshop) and a variety of bought and found woods. All the projects, apart from the natural-edged vase, use dry, seasoned wood. Using unseasoned, or green, wood will result in excessive unwanted movement. Typically, a local hardwood dealer that caters to turners is likely to provide you with a ready source when starting out.

I have not specified a wood size for each project as the items can be scaled up or down as you choose. The drawings indicate the finished sizes of the projects. So, if you are following these dimensions, select a piece of wood slightly larger than the sizes given.

I also mention whether each project is spindle turned, where the grain of the wood runs parallel to the lathe bed, or is a faceplate-turned project, where the wood grain runs at 90° to the lathe bed.

Selection of wood blanks, ready for turning

Offcuts make good and inexpensive friction chucks and drives.

WASTE-WOOD CHUCKS

I show reverse turning and holding wood between centers using friction drives made from waste-wood offcuts. I keep all the offcuts, because they can be used as cheap friction drives and jam chucks, and can be altered to suit various jobs. They are a low-cost option to solving problems. The times I use such methods in the book are explained, but I think you will find lots more ingenious uses as you venture further into turning.

HEALTH AND SAFETY

PERSONAL PROTECTIVE EQUIPMENT

Woodturning poses some risks to the turner. There are sharp tools, spinning wood, shavings and chips that fly from the work – some at very high speed. There is also dust, which is not only produced during the cutting stages but also the final sanding stages prior to applying a finish to seal and protect the work. It is fundamental that you look after yourself and use the equipment available to help minimize the dangers.

First, protect your eyes and face – as a minimum, eye protection should be used. Better still would be a full-face shield to avoid any risk from flying chips and shavings.

You also need to protect yourself from dust. Various types of mask and respirator-type filter systems fitted over the nose and mouth are available. These come in various shapes and sizes and are rated for use in different environments or with different materials and chemicals, so check that the one you buy is suitable for the work you will be doing. These can be disposable or they will have replaceable filters to ensure high performance each time the equipment is used.

Recent developments have seen the cost of powered respirators fall. These have a battery-operated filtering system and also offer full-face protection. Numerous types are available, but they all operate similarly. Again, check the rating of the filters to make sure that you have the right one for the job. Although the types described protect the person to a degree, dust and chips will still need to be removed. This can be done with larger vacuum-type extraction systems and finer ambient filter systems too. One allows you to have an extraction point close to the work, which will remove the bulk of the material produced; it is the best way of dealing with dust and chips. The other removes the finer particles the other misses.

Finally, when applying finishes, either with the lathe stationary or with the piece removed from the lathe, you might like to consider the use of protective gloves to reduce skin contact with potentially harmful finishes.

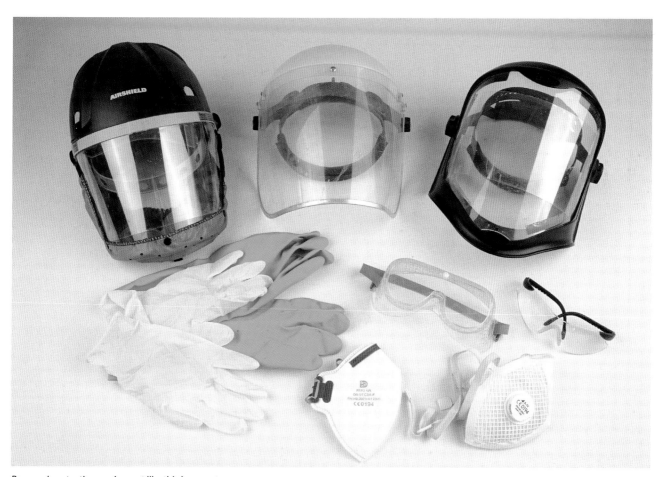

Personal protective equipment like this is a must.

LATHE SPEED

Setting the correct lathe speed is important. Set it too high and you might end up with the wood flying off the lathe, with too much vibration, or with it exploding if the wall is too thin or there is a flaw. I have included speed charts here that provide a ready gauge for both spindle and faceplate projects, based on the size of the work.

As a rule of thumb, the larger the work, the slower the safe working speed will be. In and of itself, it is not enough that the charts specify a speed range; common sense also comes into play. These recommended speeds are based on the assumption that the wood is perfectly sound, and that there are no flaws, splits, cracks, fissures, bark inclusions, or unevenness (such as being square or out of balance).

The best advice is to work within these parameters, but if in doubt – for example, if you think something is wrong that compromises the wood or has changed for the worse as you work with the wood – stop the lathe. Check the piece and determine if it is safe to continue. If you think it is worth proceeding, minimize the risk by reinforcing the piece by whatever means are appropriate and slow the lathe down.

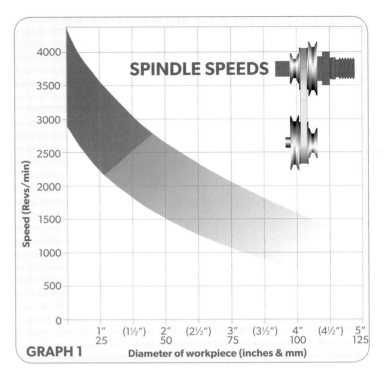

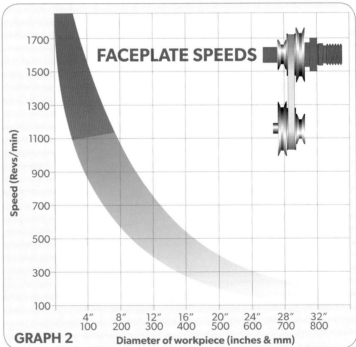

SOME GUIDELINES BEFORE YOU START TURNING

Safe turning is all about minimizing the risk of personal injury so that you can have fun. In his excellent book, *Woodturning: A Foundation Course* (GMC Publications, 1999), Keith Rowley talks about the six laws of turning. Using these rules as a basis, and adding a few more of my own, I have compiled this list of guidelines that are fundamental to good working practice and control of the tools.

- When mounting work on the lathe, double-check that the work is held securely and everything is locked in place before starting the lathe.

- Before starting the lathe, check that you have selected an appropriate lathe speed to suit the size, weight, length, and condition of the work being turned.

- Before starting the lathe, rotate the work by hand to ensure that the toolrest, which needs to be as close as possible, is actually clear of the spinning work.

- Make sure you are not wearing loose sleeves or items of clothing or jewelry that can get caught in the work. Also tie long hair back out of the way.

- The tool must be in contact with the toolrest before touching the wood.

- When using gouges, always have the flute pointing in the direction of the cut and ensure that the cutting is done with the lower wing of the tool.

- Stop the work when moving the toolrest to a new position or adjusting its height.

- For maximum control and to obtain the best finish, bevel-rubbing tools, such as gouges, parting tools, and skew chisels, should have the bevel rubbing against the work so that they cut the wood effectively and cleanly.

- Scrapers should be placed on the toolrest and used in trailing mode, with the handle higher than the cutting edge, to minimize the risk of a catch.

- Try to cut the wood downhill or with the grain. This will ensure that there is always a longer fiber behind the one being cut, giving support and reducing the risk of tearout.

PROJECTS

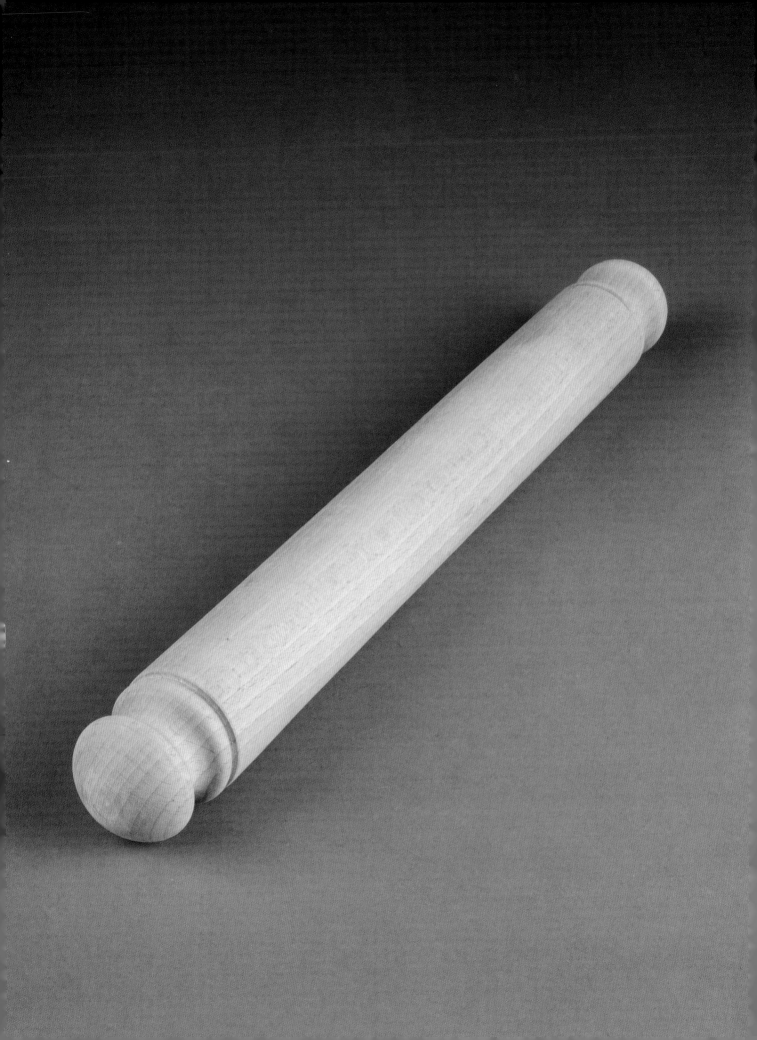

ROLLING PIN

> **The joys of home baking** are being realized by more and more people, making a handmade rolling pin an ideal gift and something to be cherished. You can probably pick up a rolling pin for a lot less money than it costs to buy the wood for this project, but where's the fun in that? If you make one yourself, you can personalize it and choose the wood too. Typically, close-grained dense hardwoods are used for kitchenware. I am using beech here, which is usually what the shop-bought ones are made from, but you can also use sycamore, maple, fruitwoods, and the like. Whatever you choose, make sure it is a clean piece of wood with no fissures, voids, or cracks where food can get stuck. This is a great spindle-turned project to start with, because it enables you to practice getting a good straight surface and creating squat ball ends, coves, and bead details.

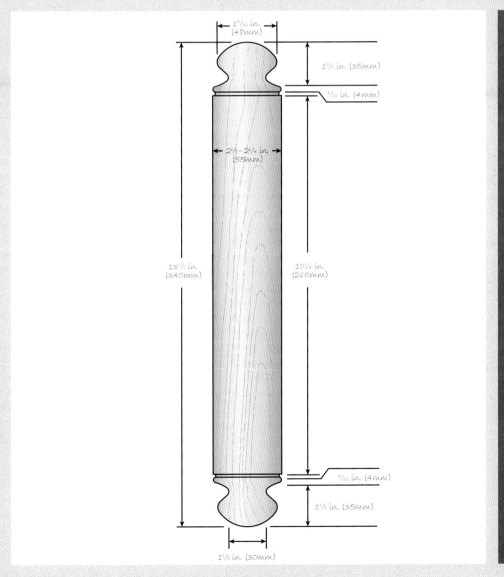

1⁵⁄₁₆ in. (48mm)

1⅜ in. (35mm)

⁵⁄₃₂ in. (4mm)

2⅛–2¼ in. (55mm)

13⅜ in. (340mm)

10¼ in. (260mm)

⁵⁄₃₂ in. (4mm)

1⅜ in. (35mm)

1⅛ in. (30mm)

You will need:

- Spindle roughing gouge
- Spindle gouge
- Skew chisel
- Drive spur/four-prong drive
- Live center
- Handsaw
- Abrasives in 120–320 grit
- Personal protective equipment (PPE): face shield, dust mask, and dust extraction

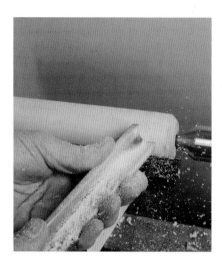

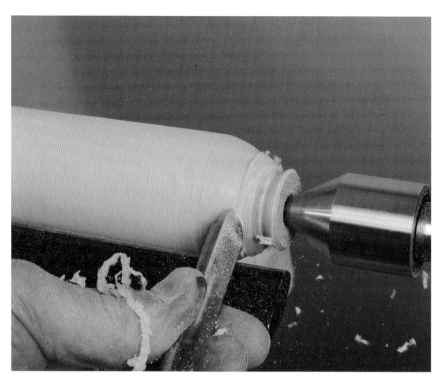

1 Mark the centerpoints on each end of your wood and mount it between the centers on the lathe. The rolling pin surface needs to be flat and uniform along the main axis. Set the toolrest parallel to the work – this will act as a depth guide and allow you to see any surface deviation as you cut. With the lathe set at about 1300 rpm, take a spindle roughing gouge and smooth the wood down to a clean cylinder. Another quick way of checking for unevenness is to stop the lathe, take a steel rule or spirit level, and place it along the work. You can then mark the high spots and micro-adjust these areas with the gouge.

2 Once you have a smooth, uniform cylinder, use a spindle gouge to round over the end nearest the tailstock. A pointed live center pokes some way into the wood, so you need to cut back away from the point, finishing up eventually with a nice clean end to the rolling pin. At this stage, make sure you do not cut all the way though the wood; you need to leave enough to be able to work at both ends without the wood wobbling or flexing. So, don't go deeper than 1 in. (25mm) at this stage – this part of the rolling pin can be refined later. Remember, the flute of the gouge points in the direction of the cut and you cut downhill in the wood, always cutting on the lower edge of the flute. Make light cuts and make sure that, when you reach the bottom of the detail, you have the gouge rolled over so the flute points to "3 o'clock" when viewed in terms of a clock face. By doing this you reduce the risk of a catch with the gouge by effectively employing a scraping cut, which minimizes the risk of a grab on the opposite side of the workpiece.

3 The squat ball-end detail of the rolling pin will be slightly smaller in diameter than that of the main rolling pin body so it won't get in the way when the pin is used to roll pastry. A cove is a nice detail to have as a visual and tactile break from the end of the main body. Measure the distance you require from the end of the pin and then cut from either side of the cove down to the bottom, gradually increasing the depth to the required level.

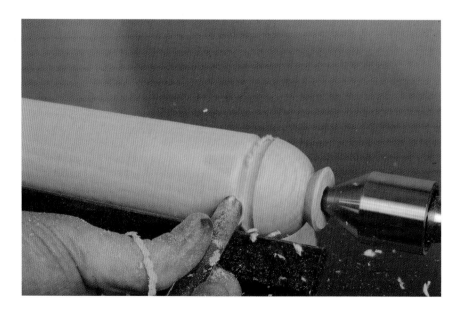

4 Again, the gouge should point in the direction of the cut, and the cut should occur on the lower wing of the tool. Never cut uphill. Get to the bottom, reverse the gouge, and cut down from the other side. Notice how the squat ball-end form has been cut short at its apex. This will be rounded over a little more later on as its diameter is reduced.

5 Once you have done the tailstock end, create the same detail at the other end. Start by marking the outer end of the squat ball. Again, you need to make multiple cuts to define the end, but remember not to go too deep at this stage. You will first need to make clearance cuts from either side of the end so you can manipulate the gouge as needed.

6 As with the other end, measure and cut the cove detail.

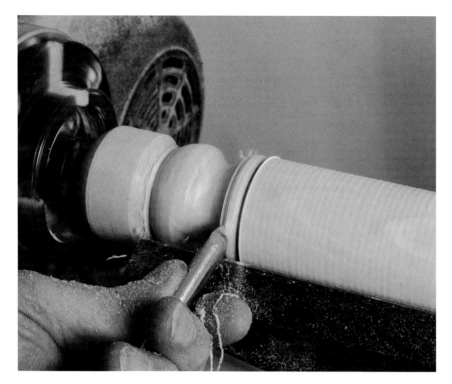

7 Now create a bead – a new detail – at the right-hand side of the cove to create a separation from the main body. Having the cove flow straight into it can work, but I find a precise stop detail more pleasing. Remember to start at the top of the bead and roll down either side of it, rotating the gouge as you go so that you cut on the lower wing. It doesn't have to be too deep.

8 Once the bead is cut, refine the shape of the end, cove, and bead to make sure everything is visually balanced and looks right.

10 Now create the bead and refine the shape at the tailstock end so that it matches exactly – or at least as close as possible – what is on the other end. You can see I need to do a bit of reshaping to get them to match.

9 Deepen the cut at the end of the squat ball-end so there will not be much to take off later, but retain enough strength to withstand the final shaping of the far end and the sanding stage.

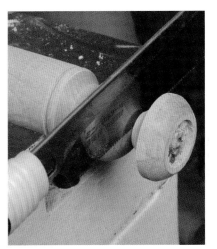

11 Sand the piece, working down through the grits from 120 to 320, making sure you don't create any hollow areas as you do so. A method for sanding the main body (not the detail) quickly is to hold a strip of sandpaper between your two hands and cradle it around the work, moving it back and forth along the length. If you use this method, make sure you have your arms well clear of the work and revolving chuck and tailstock center. If in doubt, use one hand and hold the paper underneath the work to sand it.

12 Once it has been sanded smooth, remove the piece from the lathe and saw off the excess at each end. There shouldn't be too much left to cut through. Then hand-sand the ends to round them off. There is no need to apply a finish to this project.

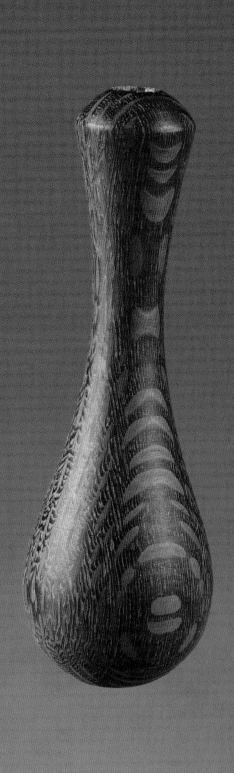

LIGHT PULL

> **A fun spindle-turned project,** a light pull is a great idea if a personalized touch is required for a cord on a light switch. To help turn the light pull, I used a cone-shaped friction drive, which makes turning the light pull much easier. Using a drive spur helps to simplify the process no end and allows you to work with a piece of wood the exact length. A hole along the length of the pull is drilled on the lathe. This is a more accurate and simple process that minimizes the risk of the hole running off-line or not aligning on deep light pulls. Many woods can be used for this project, especially hardwoods. I used roupala lacewood. This project is a great way to use up odds and ends as the shape can be adjusted to suit.

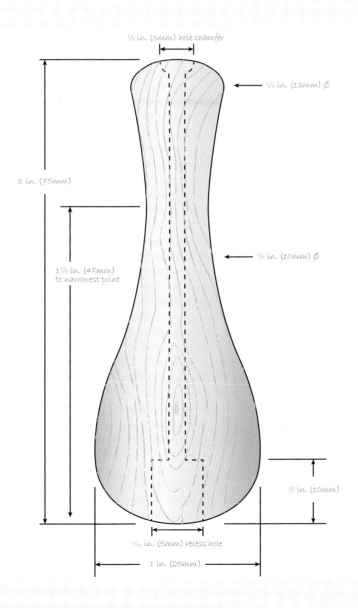

⅛ in. (3mm) hole chamfer

½ in. (13mm) ∅

3 in. (75mm)

1⅞ in. (48mm)
to narrowest point

⅜ in. (10mm) ∅

½ in. (10mm)

³⁄₁₆ in. (5mm) recess hole

1 in. (25mm)

You will need:

- Spindle roughing gouge
- Spindle gouge
- Drive spur
- Point center
- Scroll chuck
- Drill chuck with ⁵⁄₆₄-in. (2mm) and ³⁄₁₆-in. (5mm) drill bits
- Abrasives down to 400 grit
- Finish of your choice; I used an oil finish
- Wood offcut for the friction drive
- Personal protective equipment (PPE): face shield, dust mask, and dust extraction

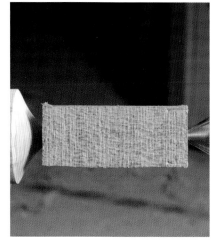

1 Hold the wood in the chuck. Because the wood is square, the corners fit in the gap between the chuck jaws. Once you have aligned the wood, fit the drill chuck and small bit in the tailstock. The hole needs to allow the pull cord to slide through it but not be too sloppy a fit. Now have the lathe running at about 800 rpm and drill the wood to the depth of the bit, withdrawing the bit regularly to clear the shavings. Depending on the length of the drill bit and the light pull, you might have to reverse the wood in the chuck so you can drill the hole all the way through. Once the hole is drilled through, replace the smaller drill bit with the bigger one and drill a hole in one end about ½ in. (13mm) deep. This creates a cavity wide enough to house the knotted cord and hide the knot from view.

2 Now you need to create a pointed friction drive. This is where one of the many offcuts that turners collect from their previous projects will come in handy. Take an endgrain piece of offcut about 2 in. (50mm) in diameter and the same length or longer and mount it in the chuck. Create a tapered cone with a fine tip/point on the front end that fits in the drilled hole on the light pull blank. A spindle gouge or spindle roughing gouge will make light work of this. Friction drives do not have to be fancy, just functional. This is something that you can keep for later projects too. Softwood or hardwood will work fine for this project. Once cut, mount the light pull blank between the tailstock and the friction drive and tighten the tailstock gently. The blank has the largest hole at the headstock end.

3 Once secured, bring up the toolrest so it is parallel with and just shy of touching the square corners of the blank when revolved by hand. Set the lathe to about 1800 rpm and, using a spindle roughing gouge, create a smooth cylinder. Remembering not to cut into the ends of the blank, work from the inner section out toward the outer edges to avoid getting a catch.

4 When you have a cylinder cut to the required diameter, use a spindle gouge to cut half a bead/ball shape on the end. The beauty of the friction drive is that you can extend the cut right to the wooden friction drive without damaging the cutting edge of the tool.

5 Refine the shape by creating more of a bead form. Remember to start from the top, rolling down from the highest point to either side to create a pleasant shape.

6 Having shaped the ball-end on the light pull, take a spindle roughing gouge and remove the bulk of the waste from the main body shape – an elongated curve with an small upsweep at the top (see the diagram on page 29).

TIP: The gouge or beading and parting tool is an ideal tool for creating beads. In this case there is some waste wood to remove, so the gouge can be better utilized for this. Start with the flute uppermost at the 12 o'clock position and roll the blade to either side, rotating the flute to the 9- or 3-o'clock position as you reach the final depth.

7 As with any cove shape, work from both ends down to the lowest point. Refine the shape, but remember you have a hole running through the center, so you must not go too thin.

8 You can see here that a spindle roughing gouge can leave a clean finish on some woods.

9 Once the body shape is to your liking, use a spindle gouge to round over the end. Take care when you roll the bead-end down to the lowest part not to touch the cutting edge of the gouge on the point center. Stop just short of it to avoid damaging the tool or the center.

10 Now step back and look at the overall shape, refining it as required. A spindle gouge is great for fine cuts.

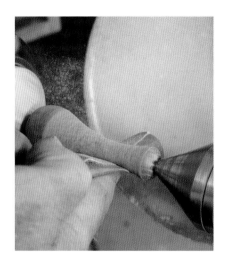

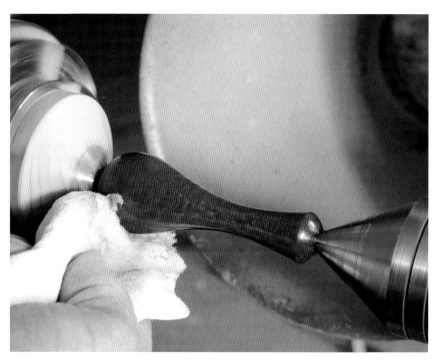

11 Sand the project to the required grit grade, remembering to work sequentially through the grits.

12 Take some paper towel and apply the finish of your choice. I chose a Danish oil finish because it seals the wood and provides a nice satin luster. Note how it enhances the color of the wood and the grain pattern.

TIP: Remember to keep the flute of the gouge pointing in the direction of cut at all times, so that the cut occurs on the lower wing. The cut occurs just down from the very tip of the tool.

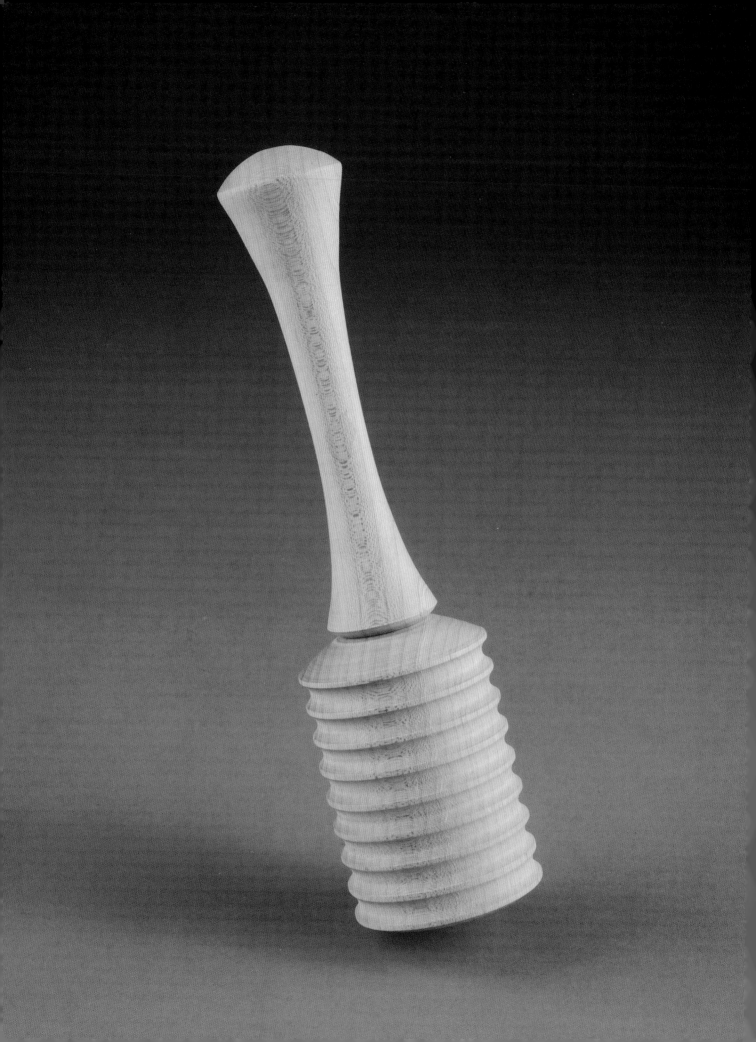

MEAT TENDERIZER

> **Although tenderizers are used** less frequently now, there are some times, particularly when preparing certain cuts of meat, when a good old bashing is the best way to make it much more tender. This is a spindle-turned project, meaning that the grain runs along the axis of the wood. The big thing to remember is to get the head and handle proportions right so you don't catch your knuckles on the board on which the meat sits and is being bashed. It is also possible to make a smaller-scale version of the tenderizer and use it as a honey dipper.

Whatever you do, you need to choose a close-grained hardwood so that there are no sections prone to chip or break. The project is designed in such a way that there are no hard or sharp edges that might easily fracture. Sycamore, beech, maple, and fruitwoods are ideal woods for this, but make sure that the blank you choose is free of blemishes. Although I do not apply a finish to this type of work, you could choose a food-safe oil or a salad oil such as sunflower oil.

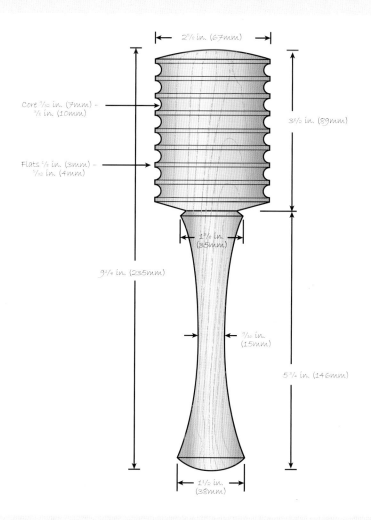

2⅝ in. (67mm)

Core ⁹⁄₃₂ in. (7mm) – ⅜ in. (10mm)

Flats ⅛ in. (3mm) – ⁵⁄₃₂ in. (4mm)

3½ in. (89mm)

1⅜ in. (35mm)

9¼ in. (235mm)

⁹⁄₁₆ in. (15mm)

5¾ in. (146mm)

1½ in. (38mm)

You will need:

- Spindle roughing gouge
- Spindle gouge
- Skew chisel
- Beading and parting tool
- Scroll chuck
- Abrasives down to 320 grit
- Live center
- Drive spur
- Personal protective equipment (PPE): face shield, dust mask, and dust extraction

1 Mark the centerpoints, then mount the piece of wood between the centers and use a spindle roughing gouge to clean up the wood until it is an even cylindrical shape. A typical speed range for this project is about 1200 rpm for the rough shaping and 1500 to 1800 rpm for the fine finishing cuts. Remember to work at a speed that you are comfortable with; if in doubt, slow things down.

2 I prefer to hold a project in a chuck whenever possible, although with this project you do not have to if you cut your work almost to length. I find the chuck hold offers a bit more security and is therefore a somewhat safer option. So, assuming you will do likewise, use the beading and parting tool to cut a tenon on the tailstock end of the work to suit your chuck. Once cut, remove the work from the lathe and fix the tenon in the chuck before locking everything down securely. Bring up the tailstock at the other end and secure it in place.

3 Now take a pencil or marker pen and mark the length of the head and the handle on the work. Use a beading and parting tool to cut just shy of the finished depth for the handle section where it meets the head.

4 If the blank is slightly oversized, use a spindle roughing gouge to reduce the diameter of the head section.

5 Now take a spindle gouge and create the curved top of the head section. Make a few cuts and create a little stub where the live center enters the wood. It should be big enough that when you eventually remove the stub there will be no penetration mark left from the live center. Don't make the stub too small or it might fracture – ½ in. (13mm) or so wide is about right, but go with a bigger size if you feel more caution is required.

TIP: Note the presentation angle of the blade in step 6. Entering the cut from the right-hand side of the core, the flute of the gouge should point at the 9 o'clock position. As the cut progresses to the lowest point, the gouge is rotated so the flute is almost at the 12 o'clock position at the bottom. The other side is then done with the flute starting at 3 o'clock.

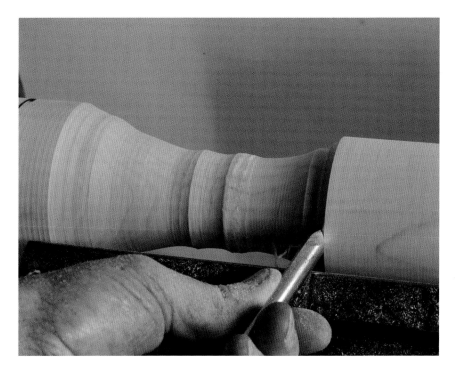

6 With the top of the head cut, use a spindle gouge to shape the lower section of the head where the handle meets it.

TIP: I have chosen coves for the project because I find them more tactile and easier to clean, but you could have V-cuts instead. Just remember to leave flats on the intersecting areas; if you have sharp points, they will shatter when they hit hard surfaces.

7 Using a spindle gouge once more, cut a series of coves, leaving a flat area ⅛ to ⁵⁄₃₂ in. (3–4mm) long in between each one so that there are no sharp or weak elements that will break. When shaping the coves, cut from the highest point down to the lowest part and have the gouge pointing in the direction of the cut, with the cut occurring on the lower wing at all times. You will need to work from both sides to do this – never cut uphill or you will get a catch and torn grain. Repeat the cuts until you have completed the whole row of coves. Try to make them all even in width and depth. If you struggle with a gouge, use a shaped scraper; the finish will not be as clean and more sanding will be required later, but you will be able to just push the scraper in very gently to create the desired shape.

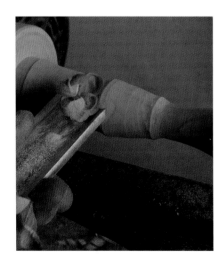

8 Once you have cut the coves, use a spindle roughing gouge and spindle gouge to refine the shape of the handle. Stop the lathe regularly to check that the shape you create is comfortable in the hand.

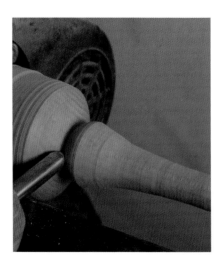

9 Use a spindle gouge to just dome over the end of the handle section. Do not cut all the way though; leave a stub of about ½ in. (13mm). We will cut this off later.

10 Now sand the piece all over, starting at about 120 grit and working down to 240 or even 320 grit to get a nice silky finish on the work. After sanding, you can apply a finish if you like.

11 If necessary, use either a spindle gouge or skew chisel to refine the end of the head and then sand before removing the item from the lathe.

12 Finally, cut off the end waste on the handle section and also the stub left on the head. Sand the sections round.

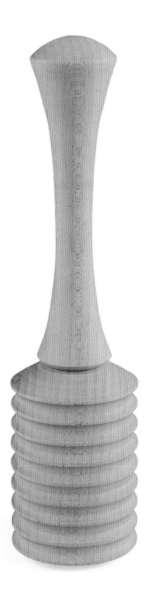

PASTRY TAMPER

> **A lovely kitchen utensil** that any cook will appreciate, a pastry tamper is a great help when pushing the dough for small quiches and tarts into the baking pans. If you make a tamper for a friend, I am sure they will reciprocate with all manner of pastry goodies as a result of your kindness. You are, however, going to need different sizes, to match the variety of sizes of baking pans. You also need to check with the cook to find out how much smaller than the opening in the pan the tamper needs to be to achieve the desired pastry thickness. Offcuts of close-grained dense wood such as fruitwoods, maple, sycamore, and beech work well for this. This is another spindle-turned project and doesn't require a finish.

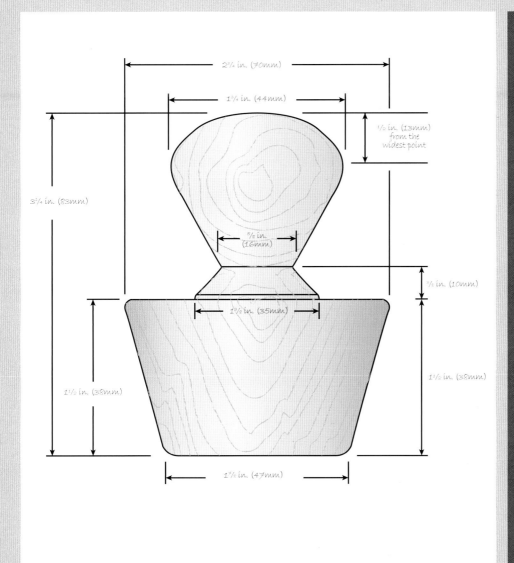

2¾ in. (70mm)

1¾ in. (44mm)

½ in. (13mm) from the widest point

3¼ in. (83mm)

⅝ in. (16mm)

⅜ in. (10mm)

1⅜ in. (35mm)

1½ in. (38mm)

1½ in. (38mm)

1⅞ in. (47mm)

You will need:

- Spindle roughing gouge
- Spindle gouge
- Beading and parting tool
- Thin parting tool
- Abrasives down to 400 grit
- Scroll chuck
- Live center
- Drive spur
- Calipers
- Ruler
- Drill
- Power sanding arbor
- Paper towel
- Personal protective equipment (PPE): face shield, dust mask, and dust extraction

1 Offcuts of close-grained dense wood are fine for this. The blank on the right in this photo is the offcut from the meat tenderizer, and is long enough to work well here.

2 Measure the widest and the narrowest part of the pan being used for the pastry.

3 You also need to know the depth. From these measurements you will be able to sort out the taper length and size the pastry tamper to fit.

4 The wood, which already has a tenon on the end, is mounted in the chuck. Measuring it reveals it is wide enough to accommodate the largest width required for the tamper.

5 Use a spindle gouge to clean up the end grain. Set the lathe at about 1500 rpm to suit the maximum diameter of this project. Note that the tool handle is held low, which results in an elongated cutting edge that can be used to shear off the end grain easily and cleanly. This is a very useful cut, especially for wood with tricky grain.

6 Here, the same cut is being used to refine the surface further. The flute still points in the direction of cut and the cut occurs on the lower wing.

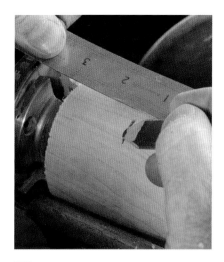

7 Check that the surface is flat – the pan I need the tamper for has flat bottoms and needs a flat base. Of course, the shape can be changed to suit the pan your tamper will be used with. A beading and parting tool can be used to micro-adjust the wood to create a flat surface.

8 Use a spindle roughing gouge to reduce the blank to a cylinder just larger than the maximum required size.

9 Measure in from the end the depth required then add a bit so the tamper will sit proud of the top of the pan being used. In this case it will be about ⅛ in. (3mm).

10 Use a beading and parting tool to show the maximum height and remove some of the waste in that area. Do not go too deep; the handle needs to be cut later, and there is some shaping to do on the tamper end. The right-hand edge of the beading and parting tool is cutting exactly on the pencil mark and just a bit deeper than the maximum diameter required for the top part of the taper.

11 Use the calipers to mark the smallest diameter required on the unsupported end. The lathe revolves counter-clockwise, so only the left-hand side of the calipers must touch the wood.

12 Use the spindle roughing gouge to create the taper. Make light cuts and try to get as clean a surface as you can.

13 Once you have shaped this part of the tamper, check the size and fit.

14 There needs to be a gap. For this particular job, the tamper should provide ⅛-in. (3mm)-thick pastry, so remount the blank and adjust the taper to the correct size. Check again and remount the wood on the lathe.

15 You can see from the pastry of this tart (which was cut in half and consumed afterward with a cup of coffee) the uniform thickness required for the pastry.

16 Use a beading and parting tool to remove the waste prior to shaping the end of the handle. Create a straight or curved lower handle section as required.

17 Use a spindle gouge to refine the shape further. You can then sand the lower section as necessary. The beading and parting tool left a small shoulder on the upper section of the tapered tamper; it is a nice detail that you can choose to leave or take off.

18 Before you go too far, remove the wood from the lathe and measure the bottom diameter. I am going to reverse the piece to make the shaping of the handle easier. However, you cannot grip the taper in the chuck without marking the work, so a jam chuck can be used to help here.

19 Another offcut can be used, in this case a waste section from an old vase project. Just mount the blank to be used in the chuck and cut a section out to match the diameter of the base. Taper it out just a little. A tapered hole about ⅜ in. (10mm) deep and about 1/16 in. (1.5mm) wider than the taper of the tamper will be great. A beading and parting tool will make light work of the cutting.

20 Check for fit. You do not want any friction marks on the work, so use some paper towel – one or two layers are all you need if you left a tiny gap on the jam chuck. Place the paper towel over the hole and then press the base of the tamper in the hole and bring up the tailstock, securing it in position. A ring center is used to minimize point projection in the wood. Remember, if you do not have one, use the adhesive putty and washer method (see page 11), which does the same job and also spreads the pressure load for a more secure hold. Remove some of the waste from the end.

21 Now use a spindle gouge to refine the handle shape. Note the shoulder previously mentioned. I left the taper relatively straight on the handle. A rounded form will fit the hand well and not be uncomfortable when applying pressure on it to form the pastry.

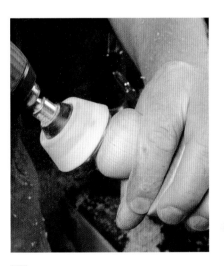

22 The ring center leaves quite a large surface section, which we need to avoid, so a thin parting tool can be used to remove some waste below the center. Part it just shy of all the way through and then remove the tamper from the lathe and saw off the remainder.

23 Now sand it clean, either with a power sanding arbor in a drill or by hand to the finish you require.

BUD VASE

> **Also known as weed pots**, bud vases are designed to display dried or artificial flowers. Another spindle-turned project, this is ideal for developing your turning skills. It can be made from found wood, logs, or scrap lumber, as well as those lovely pieces that catch your eye at the hardwood dealer's. Bud vases can be designed in myriad shapes and sizes, and you don't need a lot of tools to make them. Have fun with these and don't get hung up on the size – vary it according to the piece of wood you have. Just make sure that all the proportions and scale of the design work together.

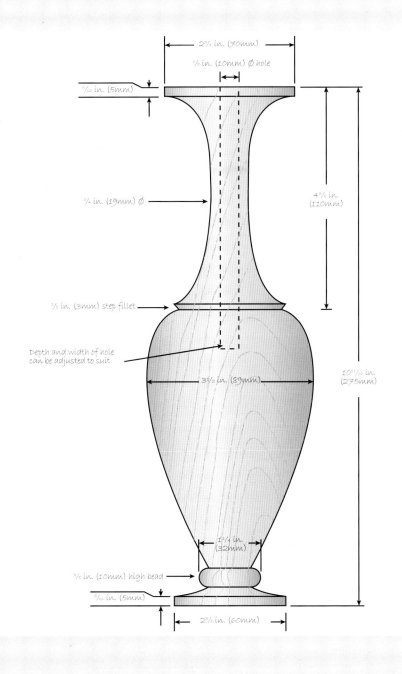

2⁹/₁₆ in. (70mm)

³/₈ in. (10mm) Ø hole

³/₁₆ in. (5mm)

³/₄ in. (19mm) Ø

4⁵/₁₆ in. (110mm)

¹/₈ in. (3mm) step fillet

Depth and width of hole can be adjusted to suit

3¹/₂ in. (89mm)

10¹¹/₁₆ in. (275mm)

1¹/₄ in. (32mm)

³/₈ in. (10mm) high bead

³/₁₆ in. (5mm)

2³/₈ in. (60mm)

You will need:

- Spindle roughing gouge
- Beading and parting tool
- Spindle gouge
- Drill chuck
- Drill bit
- Scroll chuck
- Drive spur
- Live center
- Abrasives 120–320 grit
- Acrylic sanding sealer
- Wax finish
- Paper towel
- Carving gouge
- Personal protective equipment (PPE): face shield, dust mask, and dust extraction

1 Choose a piece of wood you like – I went for spalted beech – and cut it a little larger than the required vase size. Mark the center point at either end and mount it between the centers. Secure the tailstock in place and, with the live center squarely planted in the wood, lock the quill. The piece I used had some loose bark sections, which are common on log pieces, and some burls. These can fly off unexpectedly during turning, so it is best to remove all loose sections before turning on the lathe. Position the toolrest, making sure it is clear of the spinning wood, and then set the lathe to about 900 rpm to start.

2 Use a spindle roughing gouge to reduce the wood to a nice even cylinder. Remember to work from the center out to either end, with the flute always pointing in the direction of travel. Never enter the tool into the very end of the wood and expect to cut in a straight line – this tool will grab if you do that. When the workpiece is almost cylindrical, make a smoothing cut by starting about 1 in. (25mm) in from one end and running the tool along the work until you reach the other end. Reverse the tool to deal with the 1 in. (25mm) section left from the start of the cut.

3 Now use a beading and parting tool to cut a tenon on one end to suit your chuck jaws. Remember to keep this as large as possible to provide support during the turning. Once you have cut the tenon, remove the work from between the centers and fit it into the chuck jaws, clamping it tight and secure. Remember to use the tailstock to align the work perfectly while tightening the jaws.

4 You now need to drill the end hole to accept the dried flowers. I used a ³⁄₈-in. (10mm) drill bit for this. If you wish to use real flowers, the hole will need to be big enough to accommodate a test tube-type unit that can hold water. These are typically about ½ in. (13mm) in diameter, so a bigger drill and a slightly thicker neck design would be needed for this. Mount the drill chuck in the tailstock and advance the drill until you reach the depth required – regularly extract the drill during the cut to clear the chips. After drilling the hole, touch the opening section with 220-grit abrasive to clean it a little before locating the live center in the hole and securing it in place. Use a spindle gouge to clean up the end grain.

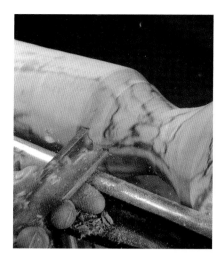

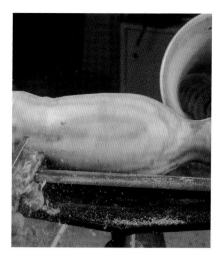

5 Increase the lathe speed to about 1250 to 1500 rpm. Remember, the most appropriate speed depends on the stability of the lathe, the integrity of the wood, the hold of the chuck, and so on. Think smart and work safely. If in doubt, keep the lathe speed low. Use a spindle roughing gouge to start shaping the neck. The wood used here was dry but it cut quite cleanly. The first cuts refine the top of the vase, with subsequent cuts working down to the lowest point. Never cut uphill. Now work from the other side – the main body of the vase side – again, cutting downhill to meet at the bottom of the curve you are creating.

6 After approximately shaping the neck area, do the same to the main body section. This will help you get a sense of proportion and balance with the piece.

7 Now go back to the neck area and refine the curve, paying attention to how the neckline meets with the flared rim. A spindle gouge is great for this.

8 Gradually work from either side with the spindle gouge to achieve the shape and depth required. Remember that there is a hole down the center of the workpiece so don't make the neck too thin.

9 I fancied having a shoulder to create a visual break between the main body and the neck but one that does not break the visual flow of the curve. A gently sloping shoulder works well with this.

10 The rim looked out of proportion, so the ⅜-in. (10mm) beading and parting tool is ideal for trimming it to the required width. A light shearing action is needed for this, so as not to damage the rim edge.

11 After you have done the main shaping, remove the piece from the chuck, reattach the drive spur in the headstock, or in this case the chuck, and re-center the work between centers as you did in the beginning. The indents from the initial mounting should be in place for you to use. Once everything is secure and the tailstock and quill are locked in position, refine the base section of the vase. Use a spindle roughing gouge to quickly remove the bulk of the waste wood.

12 Switch to a spindle gouge to refine the shape. The body form can taper to quite a small diameter near the base, although it would not be very stable, so I'll create a little detail – a very classical one in fact. This is a flared-out foot detail that has a bead in between the main body form and the foot.

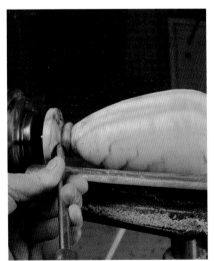

13 The detail that makes this work is the bead. It creates a visual transition between the two curves. The bead can be cut cleanly with a spindle gouge, working from the crown of the bead down on either side. As you can see, the foot is now wider, so the piece will be stable on a shelf or table.

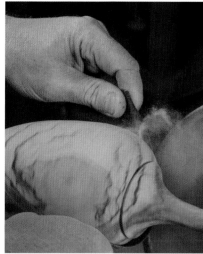

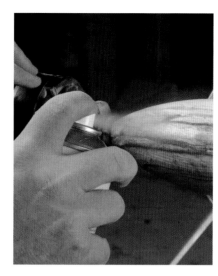

TIP: Bud vases can also be made out of tree branches, so that you have a chance of having a natural bark edge for the uppermost rim. Of course, there is a risk of splitting if the branch wood is wet. Work on dry wood for this if possible.

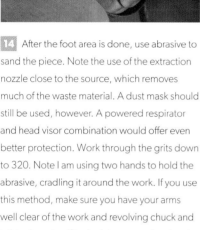

14 After the foot area is done, use abrasive to sand the piece. Note the use of the extraction nozzle close to the source, which removes much of the waste material. A dust mask should still be used, however. A powered respirator and head visor combination would offer even better protection. Work through the grits down to 320. Note I am using two hands to hold the abrasive, cradling it around the work. If you use this method, make sure you have your arms well clear of the work and revolving chuck and tailstock center. If in doubt, use one hand and hold the paper underneath the work to sand it.

15 After sanding, apply a finish of your choice. I chose to seal the wood with an acrylic sanding sealer, which acts as a base for the next finish.

16 Once the sealer is fully dry, you can apply a wax coat over it. The wax can be applied to a piece of paper towel and then worked over the running piece. Always keep the paper towel moving so you get an even coat of wax on the surface. Once done, remove the piece from the lathe, and cut off the small nub on the bottom with a gouge or knife. Sand, seal, and wax the bottom as required.

EGG CUP

> Boiled eggs for breakfast are a real treat. Dipping toast into the soft yolk brings back memories of childhood and makes a lovely breakfast for all ages. This spindle-turned project is ideal for practicing cutting. It utilizes the techniques shown in earlier projects and demonstrates a new one that will be featured regularly in later projects. For this project, I chose a fruitwood – steamed pear. The steaming gives the pear a pinkish tinge. If you prefer to go for something different, any close-grained dense wood will work.

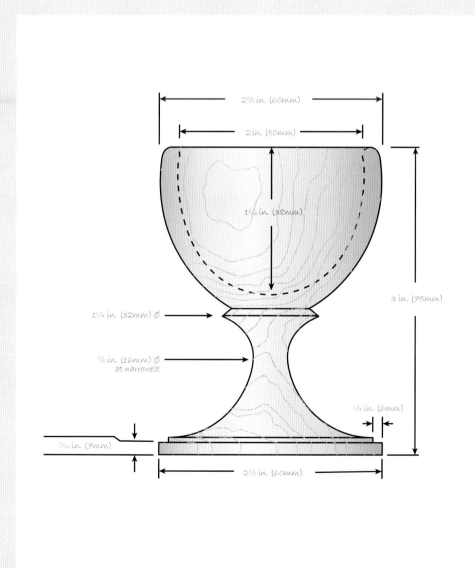

You will need:

- Spindle roughing gouge
- Beading and parting tool
- Spindle gouge
- Scraper
- Thin parting tool
- Live center
- Drive spur
- Scroll chuck
- Drill
- Power sanding arbor
- Abrasives down to 400 grit
- Finish (oil was used on this project)
- Calipers
- An egg for measuring
- Personal protective equipment (PPE): face shield, dust mask, and dust extraction

1 Mount the wood between centers and smooth it down to a cylinder with a spindle roughing gouge. Leave it slightly larger than the diameter of the finished product.

2 A beading and parting tool is an ideal choice for creating a tenon on the tailstock end of a size that fits your chuck.

3 Hold the wood in the chuck and clean up the unsupported end with a spindle gouge.

4 Carefully measure the diameter of the egg with calipers, selecting a spot just shy of the egg's widest point.

5 Mark this measurement on the open face of the wood. Be careful which part of the calipers touches the work. Assuming the lathe is running counter-clockwise, only the left-hand tip can touch the wood.

6 Next comes a cut that is well worth knowing. It is the primary one used to remove waste from endgrain wood without employing specialized tools or drill bits. Set the toolrest so that when a spindle gouge is held horizontally to the work, the center of the tip of the cutting edge is dead on the center of the work. With the flute pointing to the 10 o'clock position, move the gouge into the wood. It is worth marking the blade of the gouge to show the maximum depth you need to go. A marking pen or tape is ideal for this.

7 You must remove the blade regularly when plunging into the work to remove the waste and prevent the gouge from jamming. Once to depth, maintain the presentation angle of the blade and move the tip into the wood by about ⅛ in. (3mm). Arc the tip out from the center to just short of the marked line.

8 Continue making successive sweeping cuts, getting ever deeper with each cut sequence, until you are just short of the depth and width required.

9 When you get close to the required width, check the egg for fit. Note the gap around the outer edge and the egg. The bottom of the egg is hitting the bottom of the hole, so it needs to be deepened.

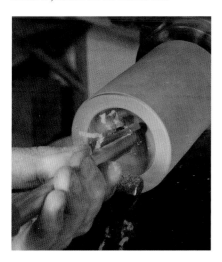

10 After adjusting the width and depth, clean up the inside with a scraper. This is used in shear-cutting mode, producing a cut that is altered by the presentation angle of the cutting edge to the wood. Having the edge at about 45° to the work gives a fine cut. Moving the cutting edge nearer the vertical gives an even finer cut, while moving it toward the horizontal gives a coarser cut.

11 Once you have shaped the inside, measure the depth of the inside cup and mark that on the outside. Remember: you now need to add a bit extra so that you do not cut through the hollow when shaping the outside of the cup. Use a beading and parting tool to mark the depth needed for the cup section.

12 The cup is too thick at the moment, so reduce the waste (a spindle roughing gouge, spindle gouge, or beading and parting tool will make light work of this) and refine the cup shape with a spindle gouge. You can shape it as you like, making sure that the egg will be supported properly while it is being eaten. The widest part should be about one-third of the way down the cup.

13 Work from the widest (and also the highest) section down either side to create the required form.

14 Make micro adjustments to refine the shape as required.

15 Remember to deepen the lowest bottom area of the outside of the cup so you have a rough idea of where to start shaping the stem. You can work part of the stem section too; this is a largish sweeping cove. There is going to be a fillet at the top of the stem where it meets the cup itself. It is a nice detail that doesn't upset the visual line of the piece. You can see the stem section partially shaped.

16 Continue to elongate, deepen, and develop the shape you need.

17 Use a beading and parting tool to determine the overall height of the stem section. Decide how high you want the egg cup to be and how wide the base should be. The base needs to be wide enough to create stability, but also proportionally balanced so that it doesn't look clunky and heavy.

18 I left a small fillet on the base section too. I found the flowing curve didn't quite work so I tried this detail and found it balanced with the one at the top of the stem. The lesson here is be prepared to alter your thinking a little. Sand the cup to the required grit grade.

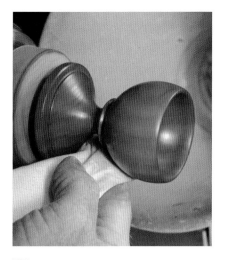

19 Apply a finish of your choice. Here, I applied oil using paper towel.

20 Use a thin parting tool to separate the egg cup from the waste. Remember to keep the waste for other projects or chucking options.

21 Once you have removed the egg cup from the lathe, sand the bottom and apply a finish.

TIP: Egg cups never tend to be very high. Typically the base is as wide as, or maybe a bit wider, than the cup itself. If you elongate the design and slim down the stem, then you have a handsome goblet design.

MODERN CANDLESTICK

> **Candlesticks make wonderful** projects – they are practical as well as attractive. This one has a modern style and is created from a single piece of wood that is shaped using the same techniques as the previous project. As you work through the book you will see the similarities in shapes and working methods. I chose walnut for its rich, deep, warm color, although this spindle-turned project will work with numerous types of wood (even pine works well). Find a piece that you like and give it a go. Make sure that you use a metal or glass candle insert in the hole to minimize the risk of fire. Never leave a lit candle unattended, and of course do not use lit candles near fabric or flammable materials.

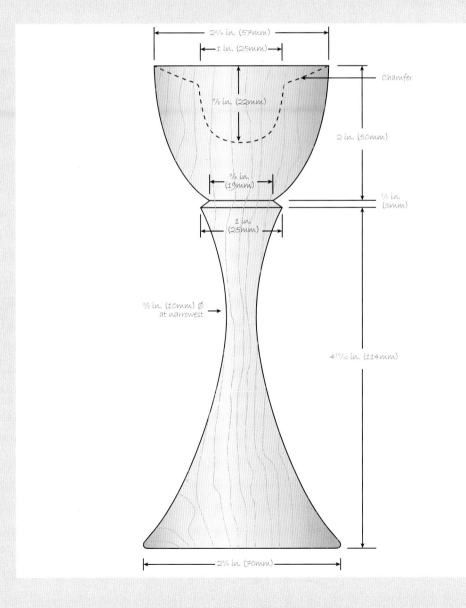

2¼ in. (57mm)
1 in. (25mm)
⅞ in. (22mm)
Chamfer
2 in. (50mm)
¾ in. (19mm)
⅛ in. (3mm)
1 in. (25mm)
⅜ in. (10mm) Ø at narrowest
4½ in. (114mm)
2¾ in. (70mm)

You will need:

- Spindle roughing gouge
- Spindle gouge
- Beading and parting tool
- Thin parting tool
- Live center
- Drive spur
- Scroll chuck
- Drill
- Power sanding arbor
- Abrasives down to 400 grit
- Finish (oil was used on this project)
- Metal or glass candle insert
- Calipers
- Paper towel
- Personal protective equipment (PPE): face shield, dust mask, and dust extraction

1 Mount the piece of wood between centers and use a spindle roughing gouge to make a cylinder. Create a tenon at the tailstock end and start to shape what will be the lower part of the candlestick. This is the part nearest the tailstock.

2 The spindle roughing gouge is capable of very quickly shaping work, but can also be used with finesse to create lovely clean, refined cuts on large sections.

3 Remove the wood from the lathe, grab the tenon in the chuck, and use the spindle roughing gouge to approximately shape the stem section. Don't make the stem too narrow at this stage. You are effectively blocking in the rough shape and position of things. Rough-shape the cup end of the candlestick. You can see how the rough shaping has defined the positions of all the parts.

4 Use a spindle gouge to clean up the top face of the cup. Notice this is the drop-handle shearing cut. Once you know this, you may find yourself using it more and more to get clean cuts on your projects.

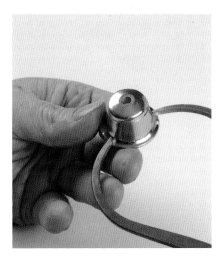  

5 Now, you need to measure the candle insert. Study it carefully. This one has a bell-shaped body with a flared rim. The underside of the rim is radiused where the rim flows into the main part of the body. You have to accommodate this when cutting the hole for the insert. You also have to decide if you want the flared rim to sit proud, recessed, or flush in the cup section.

6 Use the technique for endgrain hollowing shown in the egg cup project (page 54) to open up the hole to the right depth and width to accommodate the main body of the insert.

7 Now is the time to refine the top section. I chose to create a dish shape to accentuate the insert detail and also because it holds drips of wax well.

TIP: You can make candlesticks and nightlight holders in all sorts of shapes and sizes. The key is to ensure that the base is wide enough to be stable and support the item so it won't topple over at the slightest touch.

8 Now shape the cup of the candlestick. A spindle gouge is the best option for this. Walnut cuts very well, as you can see from the ribbon shaving.

9 Sand the top of the head and hole and radius the hole corner to accommodate the insert. If you want the rim flush with the inner section, you need to create the recess for the rim now. If you change your mind later on, the stem may be too narrow and vibrate too much during the cut to do this.

10 To help with stability while shaping the rest of the candlestick, stuff the hole for the insert with paper towel and bring up and secure the live center. This not only creates a snug fit for the center, but also prevents the point from marking the nicely cut hole. Continue to shape the stem, working from either side toward the lowest part.

11 Now develop the final form of the cup. There is a bird's beak fillet to separate the stem and the candle cup. Approximate the position for this detail.

13 The spindle roughing gouge will remove the bulk of the waste, with a final few cuts with a spindle gouge to get to the required shape. I must admit I changed my mind at this stage about the insert and recessed it into the cup so it was flush. I had to make the most delicate of cuts to do that – something that is not advisable at this late stage.

12 After you have finalized the fillet's position and radiused it, develop the stem to create a soft transition.

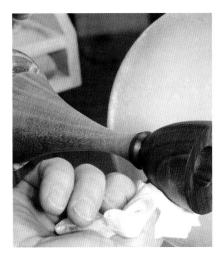

14 When you are happy with the shape, sand it and apply a finish of your choice. Once again, I have used oil to bring out the color of the wood well and leave a silky satin sheen.

15 Remove the candlestick from the lathe and put a waste-wood jam chuck, the shape of the insert recess, in the scroll chuck. Put some paper towel over the jam chuck, place the candle recess on the chuck, bring up the live center to support the piece securely, and then trim down the tenon to a small section – about ½ in. (13mm) in this case. Sand the bottom as far as possible, remove the candlestick, and carve off the remaining bit. Sand that section and apply your finish.

SCOOP

> **My wife is a chef and** has lots of scoops, but it is the homemade ones that seem to be used most often – maybe because of their personalized and tactile nature. This project is a variant on the egg cup (page 52) and modern candlestick (page 58), so you will be familiar with the techniques needed. You will need to add a handle or stem and shape the head differently, using a saw and abrasive, so it becomes a semi-enclosed scoop. As you see, the projects in this book are interconnected, so you can develop and extend your skills in a progressive way. I chose ash for this project, but close-grained hardwoods such as beech, sycamore, maple, and fruitwoods are more often used. Although ash has a more open-pore structure than those other woods, I have not encountered any problems in terms of food contamination when used with dry ingredients.

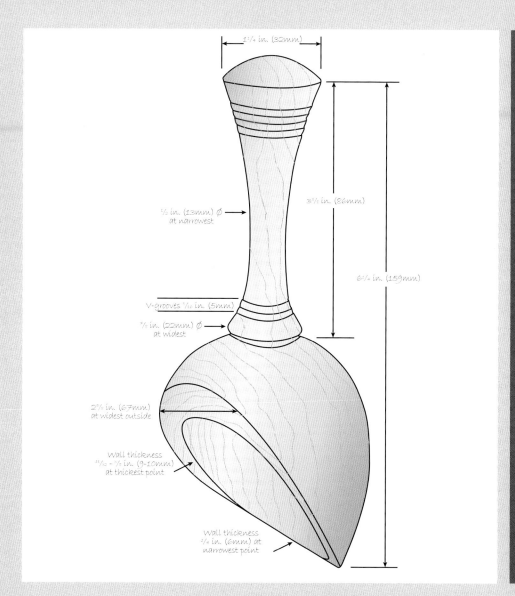

1¼ in. (32mm)

3⅜ in. (86mm)

6¼ in. (159mm)

½ in. (13mm) Ø
at narrowest

V-grooves ³⁄₁₆ in. (5mm)

⅞ in. (22mm) Ø
at widest

2⅝ in. (67mm)
at widest outside

Wall thickness
¹¹⁄₃₂ – ⅜ in. (9–10mm)
at thickest point

Wall thickness
¼ in. (6mm) at
narrowest point

You will need:

- Thin parting tool
- Spindle roughing gouge
- Spindle gouge
- Beading and parting tool
- Live center
- Drive spur
- Scroll chuck
- Drill
- Power sanding arbor or bench disc sander
- Scraper
- Forceps
- Chisel
- Abrasives down to 400 grit
- Coping saw
- Personal protective equipment (PPE): face shield, dust mask, and dust extraction

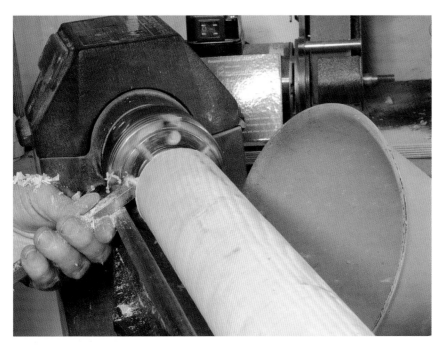

2 Because the blank is overlong, I used a thin parting tool to mark the lengths required. Then I used a beading and parting tool to cut tenons at those points, thus saving me some work later on. I then cut the excess sections off and mounted one piece in the scroll chuck.

1 I happened to buy a job lot of cylinders of ash. I do not know why they were cylinders already, but they have come in very handy for projects. As you can see, they are overlong for a single scoop – I can get four out of one piece. The first step is to mount the wood between centers and refine the shape using a spindle roughing gouge. Cut a tenon at one end, or at either end if you have a long section of wood.

4 Once you have defined your area, use a spindle roughing gouge to cut away the bulk of the waste before rough-shaping the shape of the scoop cup.

3 I reduced the wood to just over the final diameter (at its widest point). Note that the live center is used to support the work for a while. Use a spindle roughing gouge to block in the main sections, such as the main cup section where it meets the stem. Don't go too deep. You will have to hollow out the cup later, and will need strength at the back end to do that. Notice that I am cutting from either side of the depression/radiused V-cut, gradually getting to the depth required.

5 With the same technique you used to hollow out the egg cup (page 54), shape the inside of the scoop with a spindle gouge. The shape of the hollow is different for this project – its widest part is further down toward the lower section, so the way to clean up the lower and upper sections is slightly different.

6 Rough-shape the inside, then use a scraper to clean it up. Make cuts from the top rim section down to the widest section, followed by cuts from the deepest section out to the widest. A round bar toolrest allows you to rotate the cutting edge to create an aggressive or gentle cut. Never have the cutting edge rotated up into the oncoming wood. A horizontal and flat cutting position is aggressive, trailed and rotated downward to the work is more gentle.

7 During the hollowing and shaping, the inner rim developed micro chip-outs. This is not uncommon with open-grained wood.

8 A spindle gouge gently used in scraping mode – much like the hollowing technique used earlier – will round over the inner edge nicely.

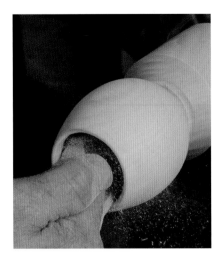

9 Follow this shaping by sanding the inside to the required grit grade to achieve the surface finish of your choice.

10 If the scoop is deep and you cannot reach easily and safely with your fingers, wrap abrasive around some forceps and sand with that, or use a sanding arbor on an extension rod or similar technique. If using forceps, hold them as shown in the photo. Never have your fingers in the finger holes of the forceps. If you get a catch inside the work, you can seriously injure yourself.

11 Once you are happy with the shape of the scoop cup, remove the workpiece and mount a scrap piece of wood for a jam chuck. Shape the scrap wood into a taper to suit the internal opening of the scoop.

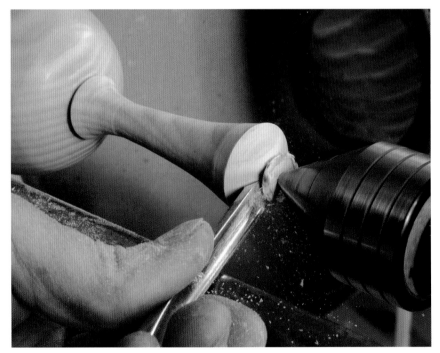

12 Place paper towel over the taper and place the scoop cup onto it, bringing up the live center and locking it securely. Use a spindle roughing gouge to rough-shape the handle. Remember to always work downhill with the grain. Don't make the narrowest part too thin or the handle may snap at that point when used. Visual as well as practical considerations come into play here.

13 Use a spindle gouge to refine the handle, much as you did for the candlestick (page 58). Note the little detail on the underside of the scoop cup. It simply differentiates the handle from the scoop cup, but it is a lovely detail and allows the handle to blend in nicely with the cup. Without it there would be an abrupt or wishy-washy and indistinct join between the two parts.

14 Be careful not to cut too far on the end section near the live center. Leave enough to provide support at this moment. Use the corner of a parting tool to create a series of decorative grooves. Once you are happy, remove the workpiece from the lathe.

15 Remove the small nub that was near the live center. A chisel and sanding arbor make light work of this and will help shape the end nicely. Mark the shape of the slope on the scoop and use a coping saw to remove the waste. Alternatively, you can sand the waste off with a disc sander if you have one.

16 Once you have shaped the scoop, you need to smooth all the cut edges. I chose not to apply a finish to this project; if you prefer to apply one, make sure you select a food-safe finish.

TIP: Scoops come in all sorts of shapes, depending on their intended purpose. Here, I have chosen an open scoop style with a swept-back opening. Of course, you can change this to a more closed shape if you wish.

NAPKIN RINGS

> **For a special occasion,** such as a big family gathering, napkin rings help set everything off nicely. They are a fun thing to make and, if you prefer, you can use the processes described to make bangles instead. The only things that change are the sizes of the hole and the overall size of the workpieces.

An important thing to remember for this project is to pick dense hardwoods that are not prone to fracturing. For this project, I used sycamore, but fruitwoods, walnut, beech, ash, and the like are also fine. Of course, there are many more than those woods to choose from; experimentation with various woods will show you what you like and what will work well. This is a spindle-turning project, where the grain of the wood runs parallel to the lathe bed. That orientation will make the rings strong.

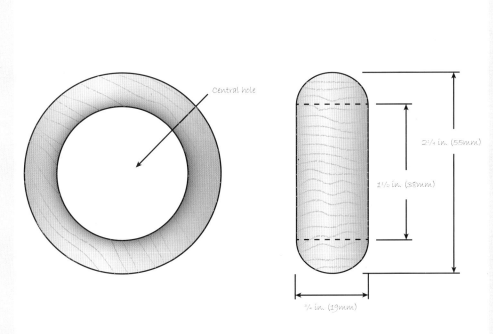

Central hole

2¼ in. (55mm)

1½ in. (38mm)

¾ in. (19mm)

You will need:
- Beading and parting tool
- Spindle roughing gouge
- Spindle gouge
- Skew chisel
- Live center
- Drive center
- Scroll chuck with jaws that open at least 2¼ in. (55mm)
- Drill chuck
- 1½-in. (38mm) Forstner bit
- Abrasives 120–400 grit
- Finish of your choice
- Personal protective equipment (PPE): face shield, dust mask, and dust extraction

1 Take a length of wood around 11¾ x 2⅜ x 2⅜ in. (300 x 60 x 60mm) in size. Mark the centerpoint at each end and mount it between centers. Once done, set the lathe speed to about 1200 rpm and, working at the tailstock end, use a beading and parting tool to cut a tenon to fit your chuck jaws. Clean up the end grain to just short of the center.

2 Stop the lathe, remove the wood from the lathe, remove the drive spur and attach the chuck, then mount the wood in the chuck using the tenon you have just cut. Bring up the tailstock live center to keep the work centered and secure. Use a spindle roughing gouge to turn the piece down to a cylinder. Remember to keep the flute pointing in the direction of travel at all times and work from the center out to each end so you never have the gouge cutting into the ends of the wood.

3 When you have a cylinder, use the beading and parting tool to cut a tenon at the tailstock end. Use the same tool to make a cut about 6 in. (150mm) away from the chuck, cutting almost all the way through but leaving a small section about ¼ in. (6mm) in diameter. Stop the lathe, remove the tailstock support, and twist off the end piece. This is safer than parting all the way through.

4 We will use the piece in the chuck to create four napkin rings and a jam-chuck for later use. You can use the other piece of wood to turn extra rings if you like. I usually make eight, to have a couple of spares for a standard set of six. Fit the drill chuck in the tailstock, lock in the drill bit, and bore out the center of the wood to just past the depth required for each ring, say to a depth of 4⅛ in. (105mm). Make sure you eject the debris regularly to prevent the drill bit from jamming.

6   Mark the width of the napkin holder on the outside of the wood, and mark the centerline position for the widest part of the holder, so you know where to cut in order to achieve an even shape. Use a spindle gouge to cut on either side of the centerline to create the dome.

5   The workpiece may be oversized. If that is the case, use a spindle roughing gouge to reduce the blank to size. Note the parting cut near the chuck to indicate the depth of the hole bored in the center.

7   Remember to have the flute always pointing in the direction of the cut and be sure to cut on the lower wing of the tool. Be careful not to go too far into the wood at this stage or you will cut through to the inner hollow.

8   Mark and cut another holder using the same process.

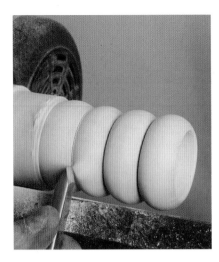

9 When you have cut the required number of rings, use a skew chisel to clean up the intersection between each one, working on both sides of the intersection to get everything even. Don't cut too deep yet.

10 Stop the lathe, remove the toolrest, and sand the first ring inside and out. Reposition the toolrest and use a skew chisel to cut through the last little bit to separate the end ring from the others.

12 You should now be left with your rings and a waste piece of wood. On the waste wood, cut a tapered tenon on the front end. The size should match the inner hole of the napkin ring, it will fit snugly on the taper. A beading and parting tool is ideal for this.

11 Once you have cut off the first ring, move the toolrest and sand the inner and outer sections that you can reach. Repeat the parting-off process until you have removed all the rings.

14 You can then mount the rings as required, sand them, and apply the finish of your choice.

13 Check the fit regularly. It should be a snug push fit so that the ring holds in place while you clean up the end of the holder that was cut away from the rest of the piece.

TIP: I made four napkin rings for this project, but I typically make 10 as a set. That way you have four to eight to use for different-sized gatherings, plus a couple of spares in case any get lost.

SALT AND PEPPER SHAKERS

> **Kitchen table utensils** are fun to make and they personalize a space. Here is a pair of stylish salt and pepper shakers that will suit any dining table and help you explore copy turning in an easy-to-follow way. The shakers are made from walnut, although any close-grained wood will work well. I used a drill chuck, with a variety of drill bits to fit the hole sizes. While not essential for all the hollowing, the drill does make life easier. If you do not have a drill chuck, the hollowing techniques learned with the scoop (page 64) and candlestick (page 58) will work well, albeit not for the very fine hole in the end of the shaker. This will require a drill bit and possibly a pair of locking pliers to hold it while drilling. I used simple stoppers for this project.

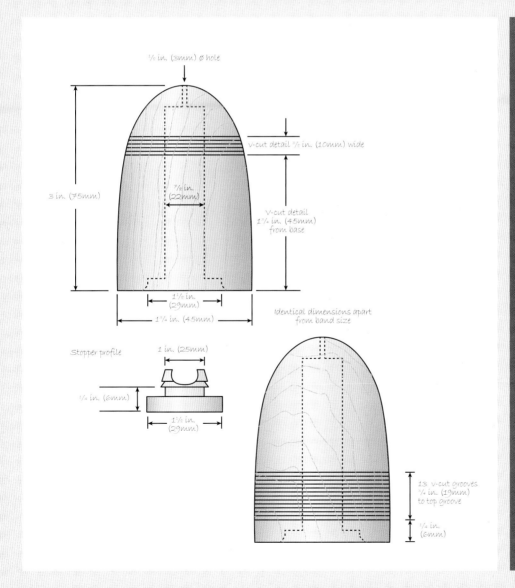

⅛ in. (3mm) Ø hole

V-cut detail ⅜ in. (10mm) wide

3 in. (75mm)

⅞ in. (22mm)

V-cut detail 1¾ in. (45mm) from base

1⅛ in. (29mm)

1¾ in. (45mm)

Identical dimensions apart from band size

Stopper profile

1 in. (25mm)

¼ in. (6mm)

1⅛ in. (29mm)

13 v-cut grooves ¾ in. (19mm) to top groove

¼ in. (6mm)

You will need:

- Spindle roughing gouge
- Beading and parting tool
- Spindle gouge
- Thin parting tool
- Screw chuck or attachment for your chuck
- Scroll chuck
- Drill chuck with selection of bits
- Abrasives down to 400 grit
- Paste wax
- Calipers
- Cap or stopper to seal end
- Personal protective equipment (PPE): face shield, dust mask, and dust extraction

1 Mount the workpiece between centers or hold it directly in the chuck on the square section. Bring up the tailstock for support. With a spindle roughing gouge, create a cylinder a little larger than the final size required. Next, use a beading and parting tool to mark the position of each shaker. Leave them about ¾ in. (19mm) overlong, with a straight section at their base end, which will serve as a tenon for holding them in a chuck later. If you mounted the wood between centers, cut a tenon at the headstock end of the wood and mount the work in the chuck. I just kept it held in the chuck securely.

2 Use a spindle roughing gouge to rough in the shape of the shakers. Note that they are arranged nose-to-nose, so to speak – I find with this shape I can see differences easier when they are aligned like this. There is a wide gap in between the shakers; some of this is waste and is where the bulk of the "overlong" section lies. It will eventually be the top area, or nose, of each shaker. Each shaker has a pointed top end.

3 Measure and mark the exact heights required. Note how I have left some thickness in the middle section between the shakers. This is necessary to provide full support for the next stage, which is drilling.

4 I used two drill bits here. One was for the width of the widest shoulder part of the flexible stopper to be used for the base. This was drilled just deeper than the shoulder depth on the stopper. The second drill bit was for the ribbed stopper diameter. The bit is just smaller that the external ribbing so the stopper fits neatly. Next, drill the middle section. Don't go too deep. You have to fully shape the external nose section. This internal cavity is the holding area for the salt or pepper.

5 Once you have drilled all the holes, check that the stopper fits neatly and securely.

6 To help remove the stopper more easily, chamfer the outer edge of the widest hole. Clean up the end of the shaker with a spindle gouge.

7 Here is the stopper secure in position. It was at this stage I realized I had made a mistake: I needed to go deeper because the parallel section on the outer face is largely going to be removed in my design, although it could be used to create taller shakers if you prefer. So, I had to drill the hole deep so the stopper would sit beyond where the part-off line would be. I then sanded the end and inner surfaces.

8 Bring up the tailstock for support – it will fit easily in the drilled hole – and use a spindle gouge to refine the shape.

9 Reduce the gap between the two shakers down to about ⅝ in. (16mm). This needs to be even and parallel. Use this time to get the shakers as close to each other in shape as you can.

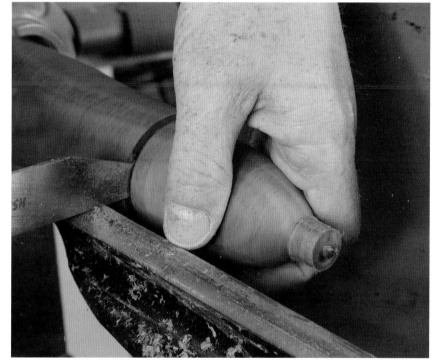

10 Next, remove the top shaker. Use a thin parting tool to cut almost all the way through before stopping the lathe and sawing through the last little stub of wood in the parting cut.

11 Remove the bottom shaker, too. Note the hand position, which keeps your arm arced over the work so that there is no chance of it catching on the chuck. Make sure you have no loose clothing that could catch either. You may prefer to part almost through, then stop the lathe and saw through the remaining stub of wood.

12 Now remove any wood left in the chuck and take the shaker that was nearest the chuck (the one not yet drilled out). Put the parallel stub at the nose end into the innermost jaw section at the lowest bottom section of the jaws. Use the tailstock to make sure the shaker is aligned on axis. The base section of the jaw opening will grip this small tenon securely while you drill the necessary holes. The holding technique may be unconventional, but it is secure and a technique worth knowing.

13 Once you have drilled the holes, remove the shaker, reverse it, and mount it in the chuck by its the base. Now shape the nose as you require it.

14 You can use the corner of a parting tool to create an attractive series of grooves. The two shakers should each have a different pattern in order to differentiate them.

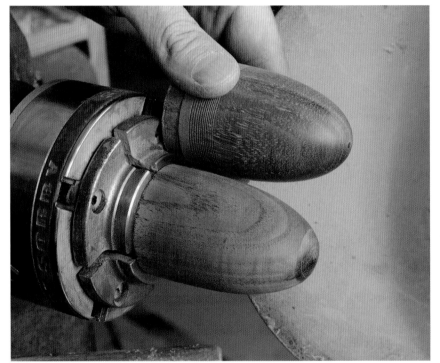

15 Now it is time to drill the smallest hole. I used a 5⁄64-in. (2mm) drill bit for this. If the hole is too big, the salt or pepper will pour out too quickly. Be sure to drill into the main reservoir hole previously cut.

16 Once you have shaped and drilled one shaker, remove it and mount the other in the chuck. Shape the nose with a spindle gouge. Again, check the two together for variation in shape and adjust as necessary. You are running out of chances to get this right, so check and adjust carefully. Once you are satisfied, drill the small end hole.

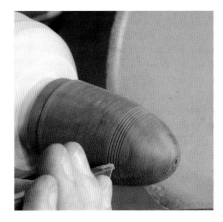  

17 Remove the shaker from the lathe, mount a piece of waste wood in the chuck, and cut a tenon to fit the size of the inner hole of the shaker. It needs to be a secure fit. Next, slide the shaker onto the waste-wood tenon and check for snugness. The shaker needs to be held securely in place. Now add the top groove detail.

18 Once the grooves are cut (this time at the nose end), sand the item and apply the finish of your choice. I chose to do this later on, with the piece off the lathe. Use a thin parting tool to remove the tenon section previously held in the chuck, but remember that you can use this as part of the design – just adjust the internal hole depths accordingly. Mount the other shaker on the waste-wood tenon and part off the tenon.

19 I chose to use a wax to finish the shakers. I didn't coat the inner holes at all, just the base and the outer section. Once applied, I left it for a few minutes and then buffed the shakers to a soft sheen with some paper towel. After applying the finish, all you need to do now is fill the shakers and fit the stopper in place.

SIMPLE BOX

> **There is something magical** about boxes. Making a box requires accuracy and good tool control, but it is a lot of fun. The sense of achievement when everything comes together is wonderful. Most of the boxes I make are, like this one, spindle-turned projects, but some can be faceplate turned, too.

I have chosen boxwood, one of the densest and most close-grained European woods, for this project. It is slightly spalted, hence the blue/black pigmentation; typically boxwood is a plain cream color. It holds detail well and is one of nature's real treats to turn. You probably have something similar in your locality, but any dense hardwood is worth trying. Boxwood is rarely available in large sizes. If you can find large pieces, more often than not they have split as they dried. Fortunately, the pith is usually dense and does not have cracks, so it will not present any problems here.

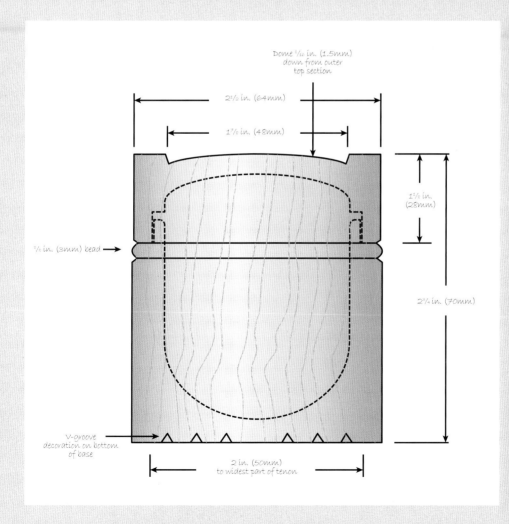

You will need:

- Spindle roughing gouge
- Beading and parting tool
- Spindle gouge
- Thin parting tool
- Scraper with round or French-curve cutting edge
- Scroll chuck
- Live center
- Drive spur
- Abrasives down to 400 grit
- Finish of your choice
- Paper towel
- Personal protective equipment (PPE): face shield, dust mask, and dust extraction

1 Mount the wood between centers and create a cylinder using a spindle roughing gouge. Trunks and branches can be so out of balance that, in order to avoid kickback, you need to begin with the toolrest a little lower, directing pressure down onto the rest rather than into the wood. Once you have your cylinder almost to its final diameter, true up either end – stop just short of the live and drive centers – and cut a tenon at each end to fit your chuck jaws.

2 Measure how high you want the box, then use a beading and parting tool to create a tenon section between the lid and base. You need to decide whether the tenon, which eventually forms part of the mating joint, is to be part of the lid or the base. Both are acceptable, but for this shape, I prefer it on the bottom section, which is the end held in the chuck.

3 The two ratios commonly used to determine the lid-to-base sizes for this type of box are either one-third of the overall height for the lid and two-thirds for the base or two-fifths lid and three-fifths base. If you are unsure which you prefer, don't be afraid to experiment.

4 Separate the lid from the base with a thin parting tool, but cut the tenon in such a way that you leave a small part of it on the top lid section. The tenon size is approximate and can be adjusted later on if required.

5 You have two options for removing the bulk of the waste from the center of the base section. Either drill it out or use the endgrain hollowing method (page 54). Remember to stop short of the tenon's outer line to leave enough thickness to adjust the outer wall section later or refine the inner section as required.

6 Make repeated cuts till you get to the shape you are after. I prefer to have a rounded bottom in the base section; if you place a ring or similar object in the box, it will be easy to scoop out. Hard corners attract dirt and make getting things out tricky unless you tip up the base section. I also like the contrasting shapes.

7 Clean up this curved form by taking shear cuts with a scraper. The one shown here has a tear-drop end. A round-nosed scraper will also work.

8 The face of the shoulder at the base of the tenon needs to be undercut by a couple of degrees, so the top and lid fit together perfectly. Adjust the diameter if you need to. A very slight taper on the tenon will work well. The tenon does need to be a reasonable length – I like a minimum of 5⁄16 in. (8mm) to ensure a secure fit later on when working on the lid. Of course, you can have a shorter tenon; it depends on the style of box being created.

9 The inner and outer corners of the tenon need to be rounded. The last thing you want is to have sharp corners that may chip or cut someone. Once you have completed the base, sand the inside to the required grit grade. A 400 grit will leave a nice silky surface.

10 Remove the base section and mount the lid in the chuck. Remove the internal waste. Carefully measure the tenon diameter left on the base section, then mark that on the lid section – it will be close but not exactly where the stub of the tenon is left from an earlier step. Cut close to the new mark but not quite to it yet.

11 The lid also has a rounded internal top profile. Once the profile is almost to the right shape, clean it up with a scraper – again, shear scraping works well here. Note that a small section of the original tenon is still in place.

12 This is an ideal time to use a beading and parting tool to create a parallel shoulder on the sidewall of the lid. Be careful not to take off too much or you will end up with a poorly fitting lid.

13 You need to regularly check the base in the lid for fit. You can see here that the fit is close but not quite right.

14 Adjust the sidewall shoulder of the lid until you get a snug fit. Once you are happy, clean up the dome section with a scraper. Also, clean up the front meeting edge of the box. A slight undercut is ideal so the lid and base meet together perfectly at the seam. Now sand and finish the inside, making sure you radius off the inner leading edge of the box to remove any sharpness there.

15 Remove the lid and reattach the base section in the chuck. You can see the stage we are now at. We need the lid in place so we can finish shaping its top as well as the outside of the box. The snug fit between lid and base will not hold the lid in place securely enough.

16 Place some paper towel over the tenon on the base and try the lid for a secure fit – you should not be able to twist it by hand when it is on. Be careful; if you get this fit too tight, you can split thin sections of wood. In truth, you may need a double-thickness of toweling to get the fit required, but if you get to three layers then this suggests the initial fit was a bit off. Don't worry – practice getting it closer on the next box you make.

17 Once you have secured the box in place, bring up the tailstock for security while you rough in the shape of the top, stopping short of the center at this stage. A parting tool is ideal for removing some of the waste.

18 Once the bulk of the waste is removed, stop the lathe, remove the tailstock, and check the lid for security. If in doubt, wrap duct tape around the seam to add an extra element of security while dealing with the lid. Once you are sure the lid will hold in place, use a spindle gouge to clean up the top. I wanted to have a slight dome on the inner section of the lid to mimic the inside dome. It is just a gentle curve but it makes a nice detail.

19 The seam between lid and base fits well at the moment, but because I made this box in one go without first rough-turning it, the wood will move – not necessarily from moisture loss but from the release of tension within the wood structure. This means that while the seam looks good now, movement will create a visual and tactile misalignment. This will also affect the fit of the tenon and lid. A useful trick is to cut a bead on the base section to disguise any movement. Use a bead-forming tool or a parting tool to roll a small bead at this juncture.

20 Once you have cut the bead, sand and finish the outside then remove the lid and very slightly adjust the tenon to get a nice easy fit on the lid – not sloppy, just one that does not need any pressure to pull the lid off. This should be all that is needed to ensure a good fit later on. Because boxwood is a very dense, close-grained wood, the movement is not as large as on some other species – experience will tell you in time what you can get away with. Now sand and finish the inside.

21 It is now time to finish off the base. Remove it from the chuck and replace it with a piece of waste wood. Create a taper on the waste wood that will hold the base. Once the waste-wood support is created, cover it with paper towel and press the base onto it, bringing up the tailstock to support everything. A combination of beading and parting tool and spindle gouge will remove most of the waste, leaving a stub at the center.

22 A slight undercut is required to enable the base to sit properly on a surface. To add detail a bead or even grooves can be worked on the bottom. Once the detail is created, sand what you can reach and remove the piece from the lathe. Use a chisel to remove the center stub, sand it, and finish off the inner area.

TIP: You can make boxes in any size or shape you need. The larger ones get called lidded vessels or containers. Chunky boxes can work, but I prefer a more balanced but not too dainty shape so that they can be used and treasured.

BEADED BOWL

> **The first faceplate project** we have tackled so far, this bowl is an ideal size for salads and fruit. In this project, the grain does not run parallel to the lathe, but at 90° to it. I have chosen sycamore for this project, but there are plenty of other options you can choose from. Bear in mind that, if the bowl is to be used with food, your choice of wood must be food-safe. When working decorative details into a design, close-grained wood is better because it reduces the risk of fracture. Also, if the salad is to have dressing on it, open-grained woods or burls with fissures and bark inclusions might hold on to food and debris, making it more difficult to clean.

It is a good idea to consider exactly how the bowl will be used and to pick the best design for the function. Stability is also important, so make sure the base of your bowl is between one third and one half of the overall diameter.

You will need:

- Bowl gouge
- Beading and parting tool
- Bead-forming tool
- Scraper with teardrop cutter with curved and flat sections
- Drill
- Power sanding arbor
- Abrasives down to 320 grit
- Finish of your choice
- Screw chuck or faceplate
- Drill bit to match screw on screw chuck
- Scroll chuck
- Live center
- Paper towel
- Personal protective equipment (PPE): face shield, dust mask, and dust extraction

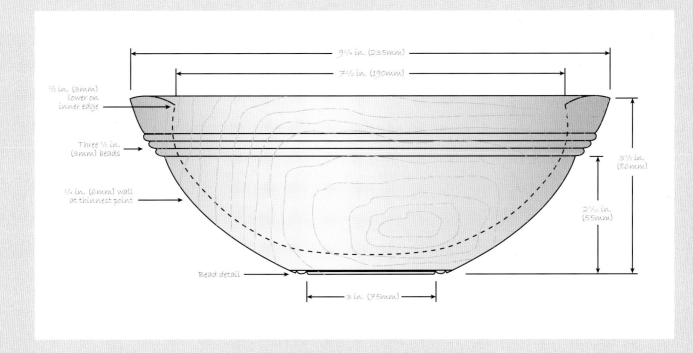

9¼ in. (235mm)

7½ in. (190mm)

⅛ in. (3mm) lower on inner edge

Three ⅛ in. (3mm) beads

¼ in. (6mm) wall at thinnest point

Bead detail

3 in. (75mm)

3⅜ in. (86mm)

2¾ in. (55mm)

1 Find and mark the center of the blank – or as close as possible – then drill a hole there for the screw of the screw chuck. Now, with the screw chuck mounted on the lathe, wind the drilled blank onto the screw until the face of the blank sits squarely up against the edges of the jaws and does not rotate or wobble. If you do not have a screw chuck, you can of course use a faceplate instead. Set the toolrest so it is parallel to the exposed flat face of the blank and adjust it so it is about ¼ in. (6mm) below center.

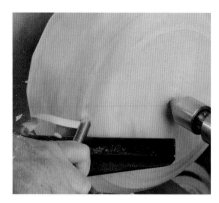

2 The toolrest should be just far enough away so it does not contact the blank when revolved by hand. With the lathe speed at about 100 rpm, use a bowl gouge to clean up the face. Start at the center, and with the flute pointing to about 10 o'clock, use a pull cut, always cutting on the bottom wing. This is not a bevel-rubbing cut, but a shaping cut used to hog away waste wood. The cuts are made so there are supporting fibers behind the one being cut – cutting downhill from the base to what eventually will be the outer top edge of the rim.

3 Next, mark out the size of tenon you need for your chuck. The tenon needs to be large enough to support the work while you cut the inside. A push cut with the bowl gouge will produce a rough shape for the tenon. Follow up with a pull cut on the bottom wing to remove waste wood near the tenon until you have enough room to make a conventional push cut again. The pull cut is useful, although with a shearing action and no bevel rub, it produces a rougher finish than a bevel-rubbing push cut.

4 Returning to the usual bevel-rubbing cut, shape the side of the bowl in what is effectively an outward and upward sweeping curve. As you refine the shape of the bowl, you'll find it easier if you move the toolrest around, to keep as little of the tool overhanging as possible at both ends of the cut. You will be getting nearer the finished shape of the bowl with each successive cut, so concentrate on getting nice smooth cuts that do not rip out grain.

5 Now it is time to cut some beads. I chose to put these about one-third of the way down on the bowl as it is high enough to see and is in an area that people would feel when they pick up the bowl. A ⅛-in. (3mm) bead-forming tool is used here, but you can also cut them with a parting tool. I find it hard to cut multiple, uniform tiny beads, so I use a bead-forming tool for smaller beads like this. Hold the flute down on the rest and arc the cutting edge into the wood until there is a micro flat on the bead itself. At this point, raise the handle to move the cutting edge from a positive cutting angle to a trailing-down, or negative-rake, angle to gently refine the bead to its full depth.

6 This project features three beads, although your piece can have more if you choose. The wing of the tool can be aligned with a previous groove to give a nice cluster of beads. Always keep the cutting edge at 90° to the face of the wood to have nicely shaped beads running parallel to the curve of the bowl. You can see here the negative-rake angle being used for the final cut.

7 You can leave the beads flush with the surface or, for more drama, have them proud of the surface. To do this, use a bowl gouge to refine the bottom section of the bowl up to the beads, making light cuts to remove a depth of about 1/16 in. (1.5mm), which should take you to the bottom of the outer groove of the bead, give or take a cut or two.

8 Now you need to deal with the top section above the beads that leads to the outer rim. Because you can't make a bevel-rubbing cut right up against the beads, you need to break with convention and cut against the grain. Lower the surface until you have a visual continuation of the main lower bowl bodyline. Effectively, the beads sit proud of the main bowl curvature.

9 It is tricky getting the two areas to visually align. Make slow, delicate shearing cuts to refine the surface and minimize tearout, then use a parting tool of some sort to refine the shape of the tenon to suit your jaws. Undercut it very slightly so that, if the tenon is long, it will sit nicely against the inner jaw section.

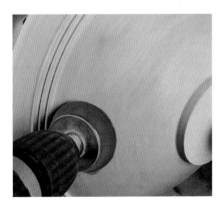

10 If you need to, use a scraper with an angled straight edge – something like a tear-drop shape with one straight side will work well – to clean up any surface irregularities. Standard or shear scraping will work well. Once you are satisfied, power and hand sand to clean up the outside.

11 When you are power sanding, do not go close to the beads or the tenon – the area adjacent to both sections should be sanded by hand. Folded abrasive is required to get into the very lower sections of the beads, but be careful not to sand flats and the like onto them. A flowing movement is required all the time.

12 Next, remove the bowl from the screw chuck, reverse it, and secure the tenon in the scroll chuck, but don't tighten the chuck fully. Place the toolrest across the front of the blank. With the flute of a bowl gouge pointing at about 2 o'clock and the handle at about 45° to the wood, push the cutting edge into the wood in line with the bevel. Maintaining that entry position parallel to the rest, move the gouge forward taking a cut about 1/8 in. (3mm) thick to clean off about a third of the face of the wood. A second or third cut may be necessary, depending on the wood used. The reason for this is to establish the highest part of the rim.

13 You will see from the drawing that there is a dome-type rim section; the highest point of the dome is about a third of the way in from the outer edge. Note, too, that the inner edge is lower than the outer edge, so the dome is lopsided and leads into the opening of the bowl. You need to cut from the highest to lowest areas.

14 Once you have roughly shaped the rim area, remove the waste wood to form the inside of the bowl. With the handle low and the flute of the gouge in the 2 o'clock position and pointing in the direction of the cut, move the tool into the wood in line with the bevel. Cut on the lower wing and work from the top face; arc the movement by bringing the handle over toward your body more, creating the curve cut as needed. Moving the handle slowly will produce a longer curve, while a faster movement will create a tighter curve.

15 Make consecutive arcing cuts, getting ever deeper and working back toward the rim. Don't go deeper than half the depth at this stage. Work back to the rim. When you reach its widest part, undercut it somewhat to create that tight inner curve. This area is what some people find tricky.

16 Aim for a final thickness in the widest part of the curve of about ¼ in. (6mm). You have to go against the grain before you can cut with the grain again on the lower curvature. Make a slow, deliberate cut without much pressure on the cutting edge, gently gliding the bevel across the wood as you move the handle. Once the undercut is created, you can start removing some of the waste from the lower section, remembering to leave some wall thickness in this area. Here we are aiming for about ⁵⁄₁₆ in. (8mm) at the bottom, to produce a graduated wall thickness. Note how the handle is low and there is a shearing action on the leading cutting edge, which is also the lower wing of the flute.

17 At the very bottom of the bowl, the wood is moving more slowly than at the rim. Lower the handle and arc down onto the center of the bowl – much like the arcing cut of a parting tool when cutting a tenon on spindle work. It is a more refined cut than just following the push cut at the same height all the way through. The flute ends up pointing at about the 3 o'clock position.

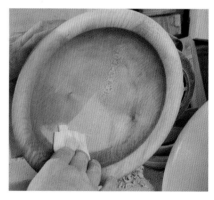

18 If you need to, use a scraper to clean up any undulations. When you are happy with the shape, sand the inside. Power sanding with a soft arbor will deal with the undercut rim easily and efficiently. Just remember to start with the coarsest grit grade to remove any damage or surface deviations, then work through the grit grades. A food-safe oil is a good finish for a salad/fruit bowl. Apply the oil with paper towel.

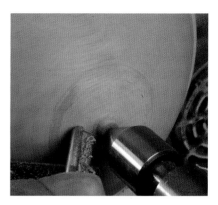

19 Once the inside is finished, remove the bowl from the lathe and fit a waste-wood section of wood in the chuck to make a friction drive. Cut a dome with a hollow center on the top face. The bowl needs to be supported on as large an area as possible when held between centers, so it won't wobble when you clean up the base. Note the darker ring on the face; this is where I want it to support the bowl.

20 Once running true, cover the friction drive with a few layers of paper towel, place the inner section of the bowl over the toweling, and bring up the tailstock and live center to support it. Don't over-tighten the live center, though. Apply just enough pressure to hold the piece in place while cutting.

21 Depending on the project, you may wish to make the tenon part of the base and refine its shape accordingly. Here, I'm making a flat (just undercut) base, so I turn away most of the tenon with a bowl gouge, leaving a small stub for the live center.

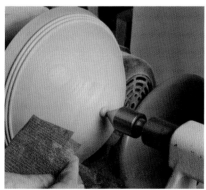

23 Use a sharp chisel to remove the stub for the live center. Now sand and finish off the bottom. Note I cut a flush bead with the forming tool into the widest part of the base. It makes a nice detail, although a V-groove would have worked, too. I like a point of interest on the underside in the areas that are unseen.

22 You need to sand the foot area where you can reach to the final grit grade and then oil the outside if you choose. Once finished, remove the piece from the lathe.

TIP: The shape of the bowl will affect its function, so consider this carefully before you begin. An outward-flowing ogee-style design is not the best for use with liquids but it is ideal for storing fruit.

MORTAR AND PESTLE

> **Herbs and spices** enhance most meals, so what better gift for a cook than a mortar and pestle to grind them with? This project consists of two parts: the bowl (mortar) and the pounder (pestle). It combines both faceplate and spindle turning.

The mortar needs to be weighty and stable enough to withstand the pounding of the pestle, and to have an internal shape that combines well with the pestle. The pestle needs to fit comfortably in the hand, and the pounding surface needs to be large enough to have plenty of contact area with the bowl for grinding and crushing. We have already covered all the techniques you need. You have created a bowl (page 88), so we just need an undercut rim on the internal section of this one and a wide base. The pestle is a variant on the rolling pin (page 22) and meat tenderizer (page 34). Close-grained dense hardwoods – such as sycamore, beech, and maple – and fruitwoods are ideal for this. I chose maple.

You will need:

- Bowl gouge
- Beading and parting tool
- Scraper
- Spindle roughing gouge
- Spindle gouge
- Drill
- Power sanding arbor
- Abrasives down to 400 grit
- Food-safe finish of your choice
- Screw chuck or faceplate
- Drill bit to match your screw chuck
- Scroll chuck
- Drive spur
- Live center
- Paper towel
- Personal protective equipment (PPE): face shield, dust mask, and dust extraction

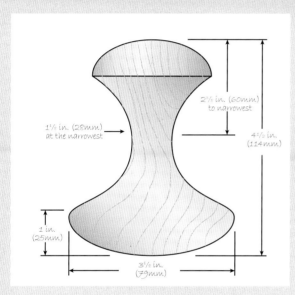

2⅜ in. (60mm) to narrowest

1⅛ in. (28mm) at the narrowest

4½ in. (114mm)

1 in. (25mm)

3⅛ in. (79mm)

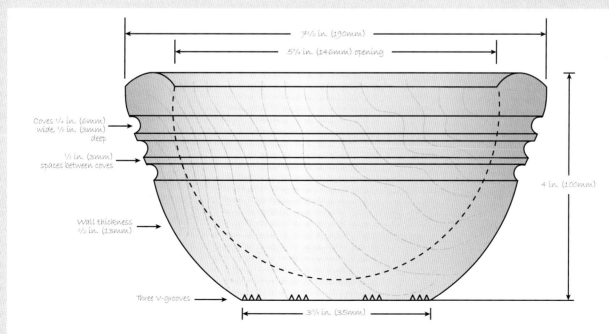

7½ in. (190mm)

5¾ in. (146mm) opening

Coves ¼ in. (6mm) wide, ⅛ in. (3mm) deep

⅛ in. (3mm) spaces between coves

Wall thickness ½ in. (13mm)

4 in. (100mm)

Three V-grooves

3⅜ in. (35mm)

1 Mark the centers of the two pieces of wood, then mount the bowl blank on the lathe. In this case, I used a screw chuck.

2 Support the blank with the tailstock and live center. With a bowl gouge, rough-shape the outside, using a pull cut and leaving enough at the bottom section for a tenon to fit your chuck jaws.

3 Develop the shape into an attractive up-sweeping curve. You can move to a push cut to refine the shape, which leaves a cleaner cut than the pull cut.

4 Gradually develop the shape to suit your needs, making ever finer cuts to refine and clean up the surface.

5 Once you have the desired shape, you might need to clean it up a bit before cutting decorative grooves in the surface. A scraper of some sort – this one is a swivel-tipped tool used in shear-cutting mode – is ideal for this.

6 Now for the grooves. I chose to have three, but you can have as many as you want. I cut them with the bowl gouge, but you can use a scraper instead. A scraper will not cut the piece as cleanly but will make its appearance more uniform (especially if you have shaped the tip of the tool specifically to the size needed). As always, practice makes perfect; just get the spacing in between and the size of the coves as even as possible.

7 After shaping, wrap some abrasive around a dowel (or, as shown here, a pen) and sand the coves.

8 Now it is time to sand the whole surface of the bowl to a final finish, remembering to work through the grits.

9 Remove the bowl from the lathe, reverse it, and mount it in the scroll chuck. Use the same techniques as on the previous bowl project (page 92) to remove the bulk of the center section. Remember to work down in stages, and cut to about a third of the bowl's full depth before working back to the rim.

10 Create the inner curve on the rim. The gouge can roll the rim over quite nicely. Work from the high point of the dome down to the lowest point on either side.

11 Remove more waste from the center, stopping short of the desired base thickness. Go back to the rim area and create the undercut needed. You have to move the gouge into the wood at a point in line with the bevel. The tool's position depends on the bevel angle, but the handle is likely to be across the face of the bowl and clear of the rim on the opposite side. When you push into the wood you can slowly swing the handle over to the nearside rim area in order to create the required undercut.

12 You need to blend the undercut curve into the lower body section previously cut. Depending on how good your tool control is, you may need to use a scraper to clean up the surface.

13 Sand the interior surface of the bowl either by hand or with a sanding arbor in a drill. The beauty of using power sanding is that it is quicker and, by using the right arbor size, you get better curved surfaces due to the increased surface contact with the work. Once you have worked through the grits, finish the inside and top outer section of the bowl with the finish of your choice. Since this is going to come into contact with food, I chose a food-safe oil.

14 Remove the bowl from the chuck, mount a waste-wood friction drive in the chuck, true up the face, cover it with paper towel, and put the inner face of the bowl onto it. Bring up the tailstock for support and use a bowl gouge to remove most of the tenon. I chose then to cut a few grooves, using the corner of a beading and parting tool. Sand what you can reach and oil the remaining surfaces. Remove the piece from the lathe, carve off the stub left, and sand and oil the rest of the base.

15 Now it is time for the pestle. Mount the spindle blank between centers and create a cylinder with a spindle roughing gouge. Cut a tenon at one end and remove the piece from the lathe, mounting it in the scroll chuck. Bring up the live center for support and create what will be the pounding surface on the tailstock end.

16 A spindle gouge is going to help you shape not only the front but also a good part of the body. You're essentially turning a large bead, albeit slightly squashed. It needs to be quite wide and thick enough to withstand the pounding pressure. At this stage, however, you will be shaping it to an approximate form. Once you have roughly shaped the end face and part of the inside section, remove the tailstock.

17 Clean off the stub that is left and check the fit against the inner curvature of the bowl. Adjust as necessary. If the fit is wrong, you will not be able to crush or grind anything.

18 Use a spindle gouge again to start refining the rest of the pestle. Note that I have reduced the thickness of the back of the pounding face. Be careful not to make the stem section too thin. Note how the stem is nothing more than a large cove, so remember your exercises in cutting coves on the tenderizer project (page 38). This cove is just bigger.

19 Once the stem is done, start shaping the handle end. This too is domed but it needs to fit in the hand well so it is comfortable to hold when grinding or crushing. You could make the pestle longer and hold the stem instead, but this variation provides a nice alternative and is very comfortable to use. Before you go too thin, sand everything up to the handle section.

20 Now use a gouge, followed by a beading and parting tool, to remove the bulk of the waste on the end, leaving enough support so that you can sand what you can reach before applying your finish and cutting off the remaining stub. Sand the stub off and then sand and oil the head.

TIP: Remember to make the pestle fit the person's hand well. This one fits mine but it might not fit someone else's. This is an ideal chance to make a truly personalized piece of work.

NATURAL-EDGE VASE

> **At some time or** other every turner wants to work with either branches of wood or bowl sections with the bark still attached – a process known as natural-edge turning. There are some basic principles associated with this, the most important of which is protecting the bark (or natural edge) at all times. I have used alder for this project. Some woods, such as yew, elm, sycamore, and beech, are better-suited to natural-edge turning because their bark is close to the sapwood and therefore more likely to stay intact. Other woods, such as some fruitwoods, have a large soft and spongy area underneath the bark, which makes it more difficult to keep the bark intact. Don't worry if a section comes away; you can stick it back with cyanoacrylate adhesive or, if something goes badly wrong, remove the whole bark section completely and keep the underlying wavy edge intact. It is a challenge, but with a few simple steps and key stages in mind, you will be well on the way to mastering the technique. This endgrain vase (which could be a goblet), made from a log section, is the perfect practice project.

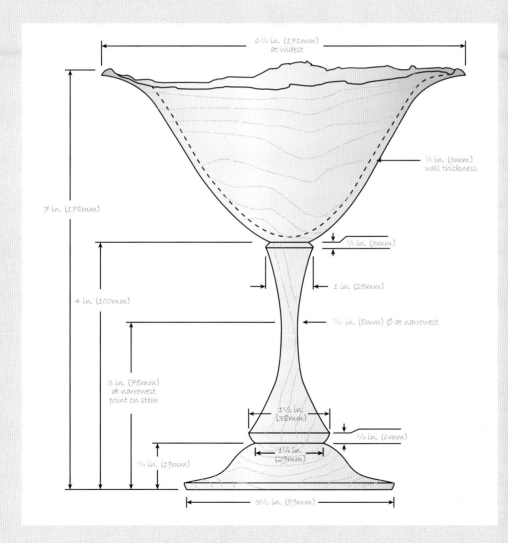

You will need:

- Bowl gouge
- Beading and parting tool
- Spindle roughing gouge
- Spindle gouge
- Thin parting tool
- Live center
- Drive spur
- Scroll chuck
- Sanding block
- Abrasives down to 400 grit
- Finish (oil was used on this project)
- Calipers
- Paper towel
- Personal protective equipment (PPE): face shield, dust mask, and dust extraction

1 Mark the centers at each end of the workpiece and secure it in place between centers with the pith off to one side. This means that the log may be off-center. Use a bowl gouge to clean up the end nearest the tailstock, then switch to a beading and parting tool to cut a tenon to fit your chuck jaws. The tenon should be close to or larger than one-third the overall diameter of the log to ensure stability. Once cut, remove the wood from the lathe, reverse it, fit the tenon in the scroll chuck, and bring up the tailstock.

2 Use a bowl gouge to clean up this end. A bowl gouge is the best tool for this because of its strength. Given the uneven surface of the typical log, the toolrest may have to be some distance from the work, resulting in a large overhang of the tool over the rest. The extra strength of the bowl gouge helps it resist chattering in this situation.

3 After cleaning up the end, use a spindle roughing gouge to remove some of the waste wood from the middle section of what will be the stem area. Note that I have left a wide section of bark near the end that was just cleaned up. All that is needed at this stage is to define the parameters of the rim and body section, so don't remove too much wood.

5 You can see the presentation angle of the gouge and the cut better here. I am cutting against the grain. The flute is not pointing at the normal 2 o'clock position; instead, it is closer to 4 o'clock. This presents an elongated cutting edge to the work, thus peeling the fibers.

4 I want to keep the tailstock in place as long as possible, so I am making a push cut from the outer edge to a point close to the tailstock. You need to cut into the bark from the outer edge in all instances to avoid or minimize the risk of removing the natural edge, even if that means working against the grain. The key is to use a gentle and controlled cut and try to angle the cutting edge to slice or peel away the wood fibers.

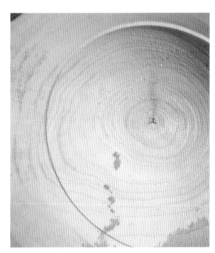

6 Technically, because the wood is endgrain-oriented, we should be working from the center out to the edge. A spindle gouge can be used to do this easily. This is the same cut we have used in previous projects such as the candlestick (page 58), scoop (page 64), and simple box (page 82). Be sure to stop well short of the bark.

7 Note the damage on the inner area and also the fluffiness of the surface.

8 Work out whether to use this cut or the one used earlier, where we had a slicing/peeling action cutting against the grain to get the best surface finish. I found that the slicing cut against the grain with a spindle gouge worked best on this wood.

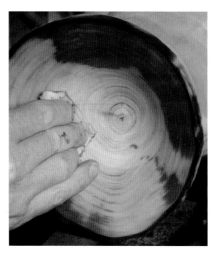

9 Depending on how clean the surface is, you can use a scraper to refine it. Work from the center of the inner hollow outward, stopping short of the bark.

10 If you find that the scraper tears the grain, go back to a gouge, then use abrasives. Whichever way you go, abrasives are the next stage. The wood is wet and needs to remain so in order to avoid splits that occur as the wood dries when it is sanded. So having decided to use oil as a finish, I coated the whole surface with it and sanded while it was wet. You can of course use water. Work through the grits, only applying more oil if you see airborne dust or if the surface becomes dry.

11 Wet sanding creates a slurry that may darken the wood slightly so this method should only be used on wood of a uniform color. If you have a dark heartwood and light sapwood, there will be color contamination.

12 Natural edges may be very uneven. If this is the case, it might be prudent to use a sanding block to minimize the risk of your fingers touching the natural edge, which should be avoided at all costs. Make sure you trail the block and sand using its lower section, so you do not have a leading edge coming into contact with the oncoming wood. If the higher edge touches the wood, it is likely to grab into it.

13 After sanding, wipe again with fresh oil to clean up the surface of slurry. Bring up the tailstock to provide support when turning the stem. Take care that the point does not damage the fresh surface. Here, I am using a bottle cap stuffed with paper towel to slide over the live center, and more paper towel between it and the wood to prevent damage.

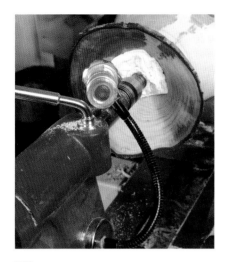

14 Tighten up the assembled parts and shine a light source, in this case a multi-bulb LED light, on the inner wall while working on the outer one. The LED is a cold light, so it doesn't dry the wood out.

15 Using a bowl gouge, gradually remove the excess wood on the outer section of the cup form. Gradually work back to the final thickness. You can see that the light from the other side shines through the thinner section. This is one way of gauging wall thickness on wet wood. When the light appears to shine evenly through the wood, you have an even wall thickness. Of course, you can double-check this with calipers after stopping the lathe.

16 Work down in stages by removing more waste and then creating the even wall thickness required. A bowl gouge works well for this. At some stage you need to determine the height of the stem. For this we need to know the depth of the cup section – a homemade gauge will help, as will a ruler.

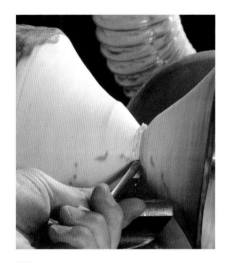

17 The bottom section should be as thin as the side walls, although I was out a little and ended up with it slightly thicker. As mentioned, this can cause problems later, so I was lucky that the wood dried evenly. Refine the bottom and the top of the stem section with a spindle gouge. When cutting into deep sections such as this, remember to rotate the blade as you reach the end of the cut so that the flute points horizontally (i.e., sideways). This will help ensure you do not end up with a catch.

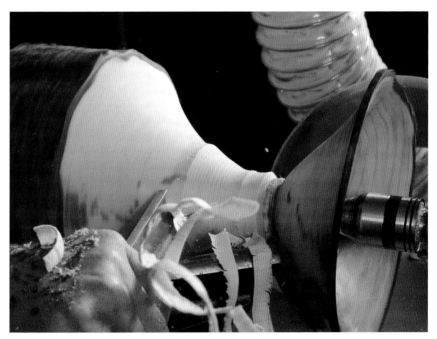

18 Once you have cut the cup, finish it off by oil sanding (as done on the inside) before you move on to creating and refining the lower section. Use a spindle roughing gouge to remove the bulk from what will be the stem section.

19 Note that the shoulder section on the cup is similar to what you have done before – the thinned section is about one-third of the way along the stem, and the lower section near the foot gradually flows to the lowest part. A spindle roughing gouge is best for bulk removal of wood and a spindle gouge for refining the shape.

20 When you have achieved more or less the desired shape, refine the top part of the stem where it meets the cup by rolling over the edge to create a rounded section. Then use a spindle roughing gouge to shape the stem further. Remember to work from both sides down to the lowest part.

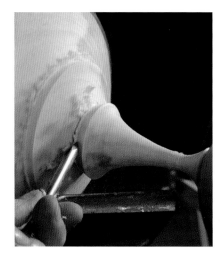

21 Once you have shaped the stem, refine the lower section where it meets the base. This will mimic the upper section detail, but a bit wider. The width of this section can be adjusted in order to get the balance of the piece just right.

22 Use a spindle roughing gouge to remove the remaining bulk for the base area, but don't take off too much – multiple light cuts are best.

23 Once you have refined the shape of the base with a spindle roughing gouge, you will see it is an ogee form (an S-shaped curve) rising up to the lower section of the stem. Use a parting tool to undercut the base part way, creating a more or less even wall thickness. Before you go too far, wet-sand the stem and top of the base.

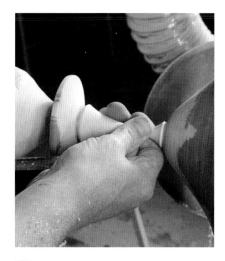

24 Now part almost through the underside, stopping just short – around ⅛ in. (3mm) or so. Remove the tailstock and the piece from the lathe, carve off the stub, and then sand and oil the bottom. You have now created a wet-turned natural-edge piece of work.

WALL CLOCK

> **Clocks are always popular** – I get requests every year for them. Look online and in the stores for the huge variety of clock mechanisms available. I bought a typical, widely available mechanism, but if you buy one of a different size, simply adjust the project measurements to match it. The mechanisms are usually sold in long- or short-reach versions, meaning the shaft is short or long. Because I wanted to use a thick section of wood I chose the long-reach version.

This project is a faceplate exercise. It is more about getting the right depth and width so that you can assemble everything rather than about complex turning skills, but accuracy is a must to get it to come together. I chose cherry, although there are many alternatives – in fact, I do not know of a wood that could not be used for this project. I love working with fruitwoods. They hold detail well, and I love the color and grain pattern of the wood.

You will need:

- Bowl gouge
- Beading and parting tool
- Thin parting tool
- Bead-forming tool
- Scraper
- Ruler
- Skew chisel
- Drill
- Sanding arbor
- Abrasives down to 320 grit
- Finish of your choice
- Screw chuck or faceplate
- Scroll chuck
- Live center
- Paper towel
- Long-reach clock mechanism
- 1 clock face
- 1 set of hands for the mechanism
- Personal protective equipment (PPE): face shield, dust mask, and dust extraction

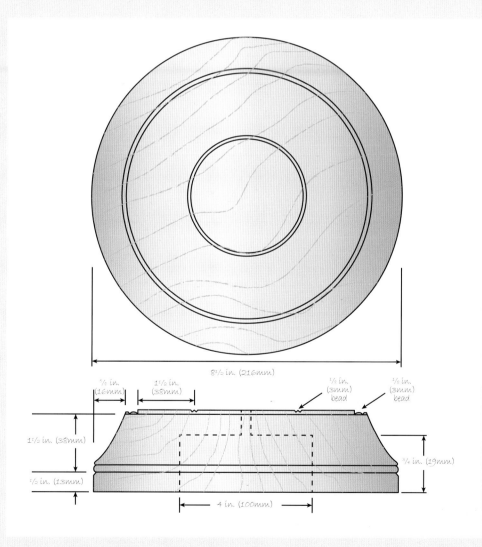

8½ in. (216mm)

⅝ in. (16mm)

1½ in. (38mm)

⅛ in. (3mm) bead

⅛ in. (3mm) bead

1½ in. (38mm)

½ in. (13mm)

¾ in. (19mm)

4 in. (100mm)

1 Here you can see the components. The battery-operated mechanism comprises the black housing, the washer, and the two brass pieces – one is a locking nut to hold the mechanism in place and the other is a spindle cap. The clock face has a self-adhesive back. The two clock hands fit on the spindle shaft of the mechanism.

2 Measure the diameter of the clock face so you know how much width you have to play with in order to add detail to the turned wood. Then drill a hole in the center of the blank to fit the screw on your screw chuck. You will be able to drill it all the way through the wood, provided you can drill square to the face and the screw is not too thick.

3 Mount the wood on the screw chuck. Bring up the tailstock for support. Clean up the face with a pull cut and clean up the outer edge so it is square. Note that the gouge is almost to the very top. If you cut through beyond the top, you run the risk of splintering off the top face. It is best to reverse the gouge and cut from the top into the outer edge.

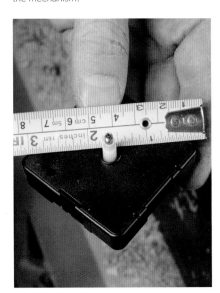

4 Now measure the diagonal width of the mechanism, as well as the depth of the body and the shaft (the brass-tipped white bit in view). The recess needs to be deep enough to fully house the mechanism and deep enough for the shaft to come through the front face of the wood by about ⅜ in. (10mm).

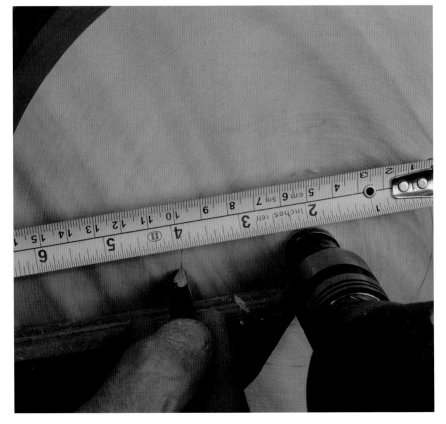

5 Mark this measurement on the face of the wood. This side of the wood will be the back; the marking indicates the size needed for a recess to hold the mechanism.

6 The width of the recess is too wide for my chuck, so a beading and parting tool can be plunged into the wood to the required depth and width. Mark the tool's shaft with a pen or tape so you know how far you have gone. I also plunged in with a thin parting tool to mark the size of a tenon to hold the piece so the face can be turned later. Remove the waste in between the two plunge cuts.

7 I thought the blank looked a little thick, so I decided to remove about ⅛ in. (3mm). I also decided to make a couple of cuts to undercut the face a little, so that when it is placed up against the wall it will touch on the outermost edges.

8 Here you can see the undercut. Note that the corner has a 45° cut on it in order to take away the harsh edge.

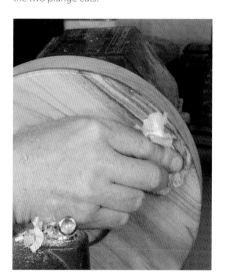

9 Now sand this face and apply your finish.

10 Remove the piece from the lathe, reverse it, and grip the piece on the tenon cut in step 6.

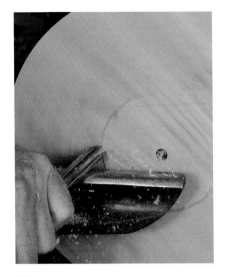

11 Once secure, clean up the top face with a bowl gouge. You can see the hole drilled for the screw chuck. The face needs to be flat.

12 Measure and mark the outer position of the clock face.

13 Try the face for fit to see that it is contained within the pencil mark.

14 The wood is nothing more than a mounting board and a frame for the clock face. I chose to place a bead at the outermost part and cut it using a bead-forming tool. The inner edge of the bead lines up with the pencil mark.

15 Now use the bowl gouge to create a cavetto on the outer edge, leaving about ⅛ in. (3mm) or so from the bead. A cavetto is best described as half a cove. If you end up with an indistinct shape on the cavetto, you can use a scraper to refine it further.

17 Now you need to determine how much you need to cut to recess the locking nut for the mechanism. It needs to sit flush with the surface.

16 Cut another bead at the lower part of the cavetto.

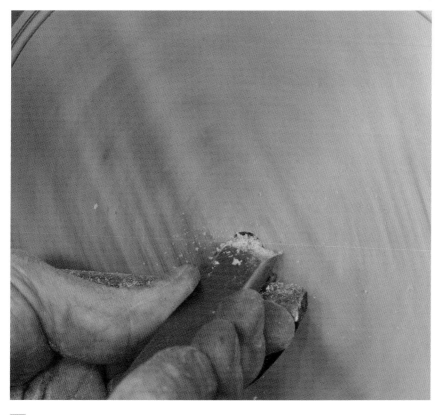

19 Check for fit – it must be nice and snug. That said, if the shaft of the mechanism doesn't pass thorough the smaller hole, you may just have to open that up a bit. A slightly larger drill than the one used for the screw chuck might be necessary.

18 The corner of a skew chisel, when used in scraping mode, fitted in here perfectly to cut a recess. Of course, it blunts the cutting edge, but it works well as a scraper at times.

21 So, go back in with the bead-forming tool to cut another bead with the outermost edge of the tool on the marked line. Sand and apply a finish to the face and edge as required.

20 Place the clock face back up to the center of the wood and mark the inner edge of the clock face. I felt it needed a bead there, too, for balance.

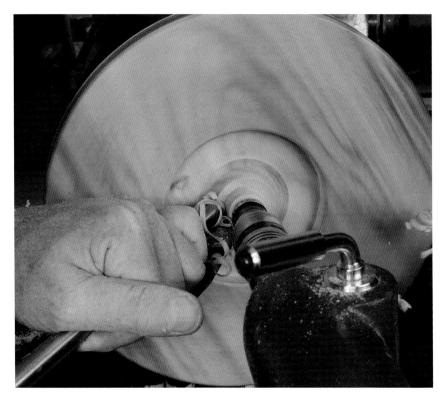

23 Clean up the recess with a beading and parting tool, leaving a stub of wood under the live center. Remove the wood from the lathe, carve off the stub of wood, and sand the recess.

22 Remove the wood from the lathe and mount a piece of waste wood in its place. Cut a flat face on it. Place tissue paper over it and bring up the tailstock to hold the wood in place so that the recess is at the tailstock end. Using the already marked center, remove most of the tenon with a bowl gouge.

24 Place the rubber washer over the shaft of the mechanism, then lay the mechanism in the recess with the shaft in the hole.

25 Now place the gold-colored locking nut on the shaft and tighten it. This means the mechanism is now held in place. There is no need to be over-aggressive in the tightening. Glue the clock face in place – there is a peel-off film on this one, but if yours does not have this, use glue and stick in place. Once the face is in place, you can slide the clock hands onto the mechanism shaft. Note the smaller hand is placed on first. Screw on the gold cap.

PLYWOOD BOWL

> **This project employs** the technique known as laminated turning and uses plywood – a versatile and stable material when used correctly. The material is birch-faced ply, often called Scandinavian ply, and the shape of the bowl is a classic called an "ogee" (effectively an S-shaped curve). The options for using plywood for turning are only limited by your imagination; you can experiment to your heart's content.

When making a laminated turning, it is important to ensure that the wood has been prepared properly. All sections must be perfectly flat and, if required, square. The various pieces must be clamped to hold them securely when glued up. Once the glue is dry, check to make sure they have glued sufficiently. Regular checking when turning is essential, and remember never to stand in the line of fire of work just in case something gives during the turning.

For this faceplate project, it is worth slowing the turning speeds a little from those recommended in the chart on page 18. A word of caution: Don't make the tenon too small to start with or you risk shearing it off along the ply-grain line if you get a catch or place undue pressure on the outer rim without tailstock support.

You will need:

- Bandsaw
- Bowl gouge
- Beading and parting tool
- Scraper
- Thin parting tool
- Screw chuck or faceplate
- Scroll chuck
- Drill and drill bit to fit the screw chuck
- Power sanding arbor
- Abrasives down to 400 grit
- Finish (oil was used on this project)
- Adhesive (I used Titebond III)
- Clamps
- Calipers
- Paper towel
- Personal protective equipment (PPE): face shield, dust mask, and dust extraction

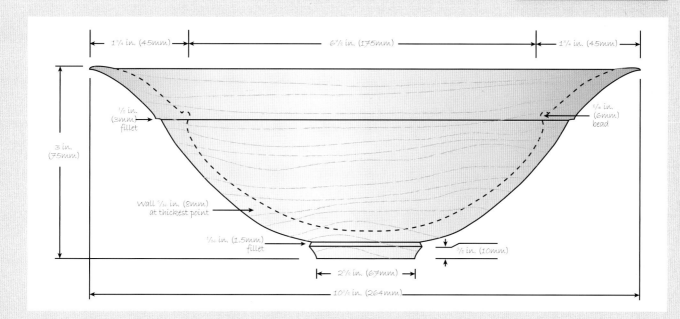

1 Take your plywood sections and, this being a flat stack, make sure the mating surfaces are free from grease. Coat the faces with glue – Titebond III, an aliphatic resin, was used for this. When you have finished spreading the glue, clamp everything together. Once dry, cut to a rough disc (use a bandsaw for this) and check the piece for any weaknesses as best you can.

2 Drill and mount the blank on a screw chuck or screw it to a faceplate, as you prefer. Bring up the tailstock for support and use a bowl gouge to create an upswept curve on what is the lower section of the bowl. The tailstock live center keeps pressure on the work and the ply laminates. If you were working endgrain plywood, a point center could well drive in too far, acting as a wedge and forcing the laminates apart. A ring center, on the other hand, sits over the top of the joints and does not do this. Either is suitable for this project.

3 Now use a parting tool to cut a recess to a depth of about ⅜ in. (10mm) in the lower face to the width of your chuck jaws – you will be creating a tenon. Next, use a bowl gouge to remove some of the waste from the lower section. A push cut will minimize tearout and create a finer surface finish than a pull cut. Because the plywood is created by having veneers glued together so each layer is perpendicular to the one below, it is not quite the same as turning "solid" wood. Still it is best to work as you would with a solid-wood bowl. Plywood can tear out quite badly, so go gently.

5 Make successive cuts until you get close to the shape you need. Note that the cut is being made on the lower leading wing of the gouge.

4 You can now see the tenon on the lower bowl shape (although there is a flat section that will need adjusting later) and the flared-out area leading to the rim. I am going to add a small fillet to create a visual and tactile separation between the lower bowl section and the flared rim, making sure that it is not so big that it interrupts the flow of the ogee shape.

6 Once you are pleased with what you can do with a gouge, move to abrasives or clean up the workpiece a little bit more with a scraper. Gentle cuts are needed here.

7 I noticed that the scraper had softened the fillet too much, so I refined it a little with a beading and parting tool.

8 Next, use abrasives to clean up the surface of the bowl properly.

9 Once you are happy with the shape, remove the bowl from the screw chuck or faceplate and mount the tenon in your chuck. Again, bring up the center in the tailstock for support.

10 Shape the outer edge of the rim first. Here, too, a push cut works well. The outer rim is just a gentle rolled-over section to soften the outer part.

11 Now create the inner section of the rim. This too is an S-section that at its innermost point terminates with a small bead-like form – something we will create later. For now, just create the main shape and make a slight up-turn at the end of the cut where the bead form will be.

12 Somewhat contrary to received wisdom (because I like the tailstock in place for as long as possible), I am going to make push cuts into the wood to remove some waste. You can make successively deeper cuts as you go toward the center, which makes the work go quickly. Remember not to completely remove the upturn on the inner rim.

13 Work back toward the center section.

14 Now go back to a conventional push cut, working from the slight upturn and toward the lower inner center.

15 Move the tailstock completely out of the way. Now use a similar cut to the ones used in step 12 to remove the center pillar left from previous shaping. Then use a push cut to refine the inner curve and depth. Use the gouge to shape the small bead form and make a final cut on the inside bowl section to clean everything nicely. Note how the bevel of the gouge is gliding across the surface of the bowl during the cut.

16 When you are satisfied with the shape, use a scraper to refine the surface further or use abrasives as required. In this case, I used a scraper followed by abrasives.

17 Once the bowl is perfectly smooth, apply the finish of your choice. I chose an oil, which I applied with a paper towel. Once done, remove the bowl from the chuck.

18 Now, fit a waste-wood section in the chuck, true it up – exactly the same as with the final stages on the beaded bowl – and use this as a jam chuck for the bowl. Remember to shield the top face with paper towel before putting the bowl in place and bringing up a live center in the tailstock for support. I used a spindle gouge with a maximum of ¾-in. (19mm) projection over the rest. Its shape is ideal for removing the grip marks from the chuck jaws. Gently cut a chamfer on the edge of the tenon and slightly undercut the base, leaving a stub where the live center is. Once you are happy with the shape, sand it and apply the finish to the outer surface. Lastly, remove the bowl, cut off the stub, sand it, and finish the base.

TWO-PART VASE

> **The shape of this piece** has its roots in ancient Roman vases I saw in the British Museum in London. It is made in two parts so you do not need special tools to work through tiny holes, although you will need a tidy meeting point to disguise the seam.

You now have all the spindle-turning skills needed for this. The techniques for the inside are the same as for the hollowing out of the scoop (page 64), and shaping the outside is no different from shaping the modern candlestick (page 58). The joint is just an extension of what you have done on a box. I have chosen sycamore, but any close-grained wood that does not have a very pronounced, wavy grain pattern will work well. If you have a wild grain pattern, it will be difficult to ensure continuity of the grain pattern at the joint.

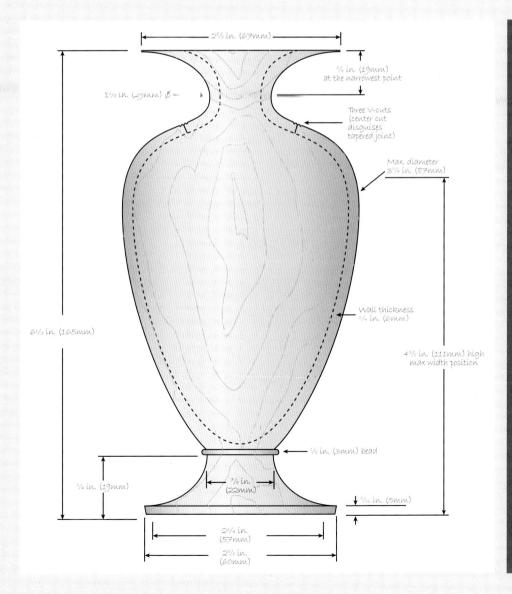

2⅝ in. (67mm)

¾ in. (19mm) at the narrowest point

1⅛ in. (29mm) ⌀

Three V-cuts (center cut disguises tapered joint)

Max. diameter 3⅜ in. (87mm)

Wall thickness ¼ in. (6mm)

6½ in. (165mm)

4⅜ in. (111mm) high max width position

⅛ in. (3mm) bead

¾ in. (19mm)

⅞ in. (22mm)

³⁄₁₆ in. (5mm)

2¼ in. (57mm)

2⅜ in. (60mm)

You will need:

- Spindle roughing gouge
- Spindle gouge
- Beading and parting tool
- Thin parting tool
- Scraper with rounded or French-curve cutting edge
- Scroll chuck
- Forceps
- Live center
- Drive spur
- Duct tape
- Abrasives down to 400 grit
- Finish of your choice
- Personal protective equipment (PPE): face shield, dust mask, and dust extraction

1 Mount the wood between the centers, clean up one end, and cut a tenon on it. Mount that end in your chuck. Use a spindle roughing gouge to create a cylinder and to block in all the major areas. On my piece, the end nearest the tailstock had a split in it. Thankfully the wood was overlong, so I could remove the split without causing problems.

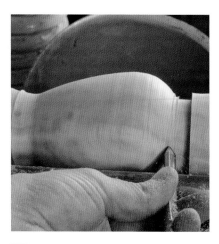

2 Don't make the lower part too thin, or it will not have enough strength when you begin to hollow out the form. Use a beading and parting tool to create the tenon on what will be the top rim section, which will fit into the lower part of the vase. Use a spindle gouge to refine the body shape near what will be the opening.

3 Use a beading and parting tool to cut another tenon at the top so that it fits the jaws on the tailstock end. With a thin parting tool, remove the top from the bottom, leaving the main part of the tenon on the top section and a small indicator section of the tenon just cut on the body part of the vase. This will tell you roughly the size of the opening hole in the main body.

4 Using either a drill or the spindle gouge, remove the bulk of the waste on the inside.

5 The overhang of the spindle gouge may cause some vibration, so use either a thicker gouge or a scraper to refine the inner hollow. Remember to work from the top to the bottom in sections so that you achieve the required wall thickness at the top first, before you finish off the bottom. Cut with the grain at all times when a smooth surface is required.

6 A round- or flat-shanked tipped tool is ideally suited for this task because it gives a bit more stability than a round bar tool. Given the gentle curve of the shape, an ordinary style of scraper will go everywhere you need on the internal hollow of this project. Don't cut to the final wall thickness, though. Go slightly oversize now, because you will skim and refine the outer profile later.

7 At the lower section, you need to work from the center out up to the widest part. Note that we have so far stayed clear of the tenon line you can see on the rim area. Leave plenty of room clear so you know you have a big enough tenon to get an accurate fit.

8 Use a spindle gouge to refine this top curve. You can now remove the tenon line indicator and create a very slight taper on the opening that is wider at the top than the bottom.

9 Sand the inside if you like. I used a pair of forceps to hold the abrasive, making sure not to put my fingers inside the finger holes, so that they wouldn't get caught if the forceps hit a catch. In fact, the hole in the rim section is so small no one can feel inside, but I still think it is worth sanding everything to a fine grit grade.

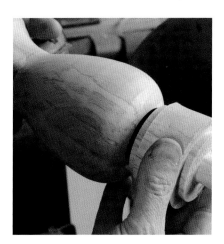

10 You can see here there is plenty of tenon on the lid part to help get an accurate fit.

11 Remove the base section and fit what will be the lid end in the chuck. It needs a small hole down the center. A spindle gouge is ideal for creating this.

12 Use a spindle gouge to create a smooth curve leading into the hole. It is the normal gouge hollowing technique, so you end up creating a radius on the inner edge of the tenon.

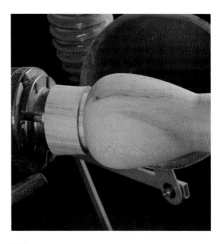

13 Measure the opening of the base section and then transfer that measurement to mark the top of the piece.

14 Use a beading and parting tool to reduce the overall tenon width, but create a taper so that the front is narrower than the back. You need to match the taper on the main body.

15 Check regularly for fit, making sure the front end of the taper fits in the hole without any gaps.

17 Once the glue has set, use a spindle gouge to remove the waste. As you can see, there is an overhang at the moment, so take gentle cuts.

16 You need to get the taper to fit into the hole with the same wall thickness as you have on the top of the vase form. Rough in the curve on the lid. Once you are happy, check the grain alignment of the lid to the main section, mark it if necessary, and apply glue around the hole opening. Bring up the tailstock to center and hold the two pieces in place while the glue sets.

18 Refine the shape, but don't remove too much from the surface. Aim for a flowing curve.

19 You can see how the tapered tenon nestles below the top surface.

20 Remove the piece from the lathe and check to see that the curves flow together.

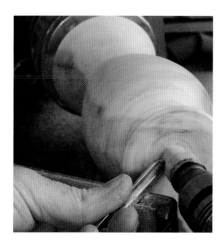

21 Fit the base tenon in the chuck, then bring up the tailstock for support and remove the tenon from the top end of the vase. Be careful near the live center, because there is a hole right through the top.

22 Use either the drop-handle peeling cut shown in the natural-edge vase project (page 103) or the standard pull hollowing cut to create an upswept curve to the rim from the hole.

23 Remove the waste on the lower section, using a combination of spindle roughing gouge followed by a spindle gouge as you go deeper.

24 Before the lower end becomes too weak to support anything done on the top end, use the corner of a parting tool to cut three evenly spaced grooves, one of which is directly on the seam between base and lid. If the lid and body fit well, this groove on the glue line will disguise the joint.

25 Now go back to the lower section. The bottom of the body form has a bead, which is the meeting point with the base but should link visually through the bead with the upper bodyline. A bead-forming tool, a spindle gouge, or a parting tool will work in this space to cut the bead. I used a bead-forming tool.

26 Once you have cut this bead, shape the foot area that sweeps up to the bead. The foot size must be enough to provide stability, but not look too big, thus making the piece look heavy.

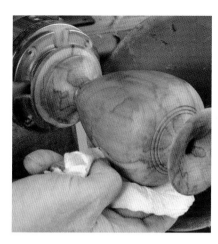 

27 Sand the vase and apply your finish. I chose oil again. Once this has been done, part the piece off from the waste wood.

28 Remove the little stub left from parting off and sand the bottom of the foot clean before oiling it.

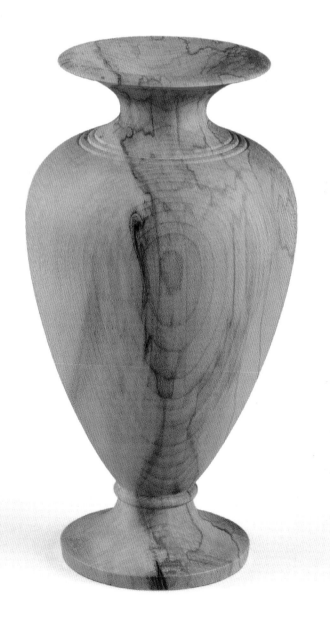

TIP: If you are looking for inspiration of what shapes to make, take a look at the tried and tested shapes used in ancient or modern pottery, ceramics, or glass.

TWO-PART CANDLESTICK

> **This interpretation of** a classical two-part candlestick involves some faceplate and spindle work, for which you now have the skills. You will have noticed that everything covered so far – assuming you started with project one – is linked and is a natural progression. Once you have mastered the basics, you will begin to see similarities between the various styles and techniques. If you get concerned about not being able to do something, just break it down into the key stages. I bet you will find that you already know how to do the component parts. Most things are a change in shape or size, but not much different in how they are tackled. Many old candlesticks were made from oak, so that's what I chose for this project.

You will need:

- Spindle roughing gouge
- Spindle gouge
- Beading and parting tool
- Thin parting tool
- Skew chisel
- Bowl gouge
- French-curve scraper or one with a teardrop cutter
- Scroll chuck
- Screw chuck or faceplate
- Drill chuck with bit
- Drive spur
- Live center
- Abrasives down to 400 grit
- Paper towel
- Finish of your choice (I chose wax)
- Metal or glass candle insert
- Adhesive (I used cyanoacrylate)
- Personal protective equipment (PPE): face shield, dust mask, and dust extraction

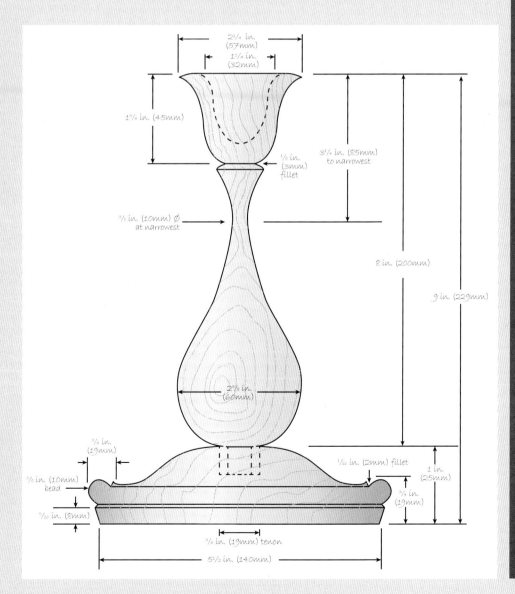

2¼ in. (57mm)
1¼ in. (32mm)
1¾ in. (45mm)
⅛ in. (3mm) fillet
3¼ in. (85mm) to narrowest
⅜ in. (10mm) Ø at narrowest
8 in. (200mm)
9 in. (229mm)
2⅜ in. (60mm)
¾ in. (19mm)
1/16 in. (2mm) fillet
⅜ in. (10mm) bead
1 in. (25mm)
¾ in. (19mm)
5/16 in. (8mm)
¾ in. (19mm) tenon
5½ in. (140mm)

1 Mark the centers of both workpieces, then mount the blank for the base between centers. My drive spur fits in the chuck. The blank is small so, mounted this way, it should be stable enough for you to use a pull cut on what will eventually be the base surface to clean it up and create a tenon to fit your chuck jaws.

2 Clean away the remaining waste area of the base so that you have a flat face or a very slight undercut.

3 While the drive centers are loaded, mount the spindle piece and turn it to a cylinder with a spindle roughing gouge . Cut a tenon at one end to fit your chuck jaws. A beading and parting tool is excellent for this.

5 Now you can either drill or use a gouge and a beading and parting tool to cut the middle hole to the right size. To be honest, the size isn't critical; it just needs to be large enough to provide stability when the shaft is glued in. Don't go too far – you don't need to go all the way through the base.

4 Remove the cylinder from the lathe and mount the base section in the scroll chuck. Clean up the out-of-balance outer edge of the piece and turn it down close to its final size.

6 There is an outer beaded area, for which I chose to use a beading and parting tool to plunge-cut into the face (there is no bevel rubbing, so it is a scrape cut) in order to set the parameters of the bead.

7 Shape the bead with a beading and parting tool, bowl gouge, or scraper.

8 Once you have formed the bead, change to a bowl gouge to create the inner detail. This is an S-curve with a slight kick up toward the bead. You can work down and across from the hole, stopping short of the bead, where there will be a fillet. This can be either flat or angled and can be refined as required.

9 If necessary, use a scraper to clean up the surface. This one has a teardrop cutter tip. Either conventional or shear cutting can be used prior to sanding the surface.

10 To finish the surface, I would advise applying the wax finish with a paper towel and buffing it off when dry. You can use various finishes for this project.

11 It is now time to shape the central stem of the candlestick. Mount the cylinder in the chuck on the tenon already cut. Either drill or cut a hole in the tailstock end to fit your candle insert.

12 You need to try the insert in order to check depth and fit.

13 The top can now be cleaned up and shaped with a spindle gouge. You can use the slow traverse low-handled shear cut featured in earlier projects. The top of this project is domed. It is slightly wide in this area at this stage, but you can get close to the final shape and the top section of the dome.

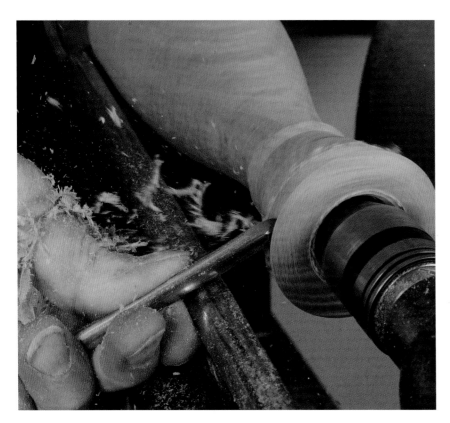

15 The head shape is much like that of a tulip flower (an S-curve). Because this section is spindle grain, work from the highest to lowest section. Don't cut too deep, or you could cut through into the hole.

14 Bring up the tailstock to support the cylinder. Use a spindle roughing gouge to partially shape the main body of the stem and reduce the diameter of the top section somewhat before moving to a spindle gouge to shape the head of the candlestick.

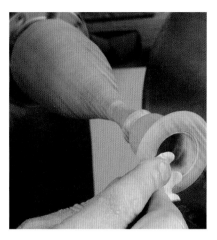

16 At the point where the head meets the stem – the stem being another S-curve – I have used another fillet to create the appearance of the cup sitting on the stem while clearly being visually linked. A spindle gouge is ideal for this, followed by a spindle roughing gouge to further rough-shape the main stem – don't go too thin yet.

17 You can see from the side view all the shapes and detail coming together. Use the spindle gouge to refine and alter the stem as you choose. Whatever you do, the flow of the main section into the cup head needs to be sinuous, without jarring transitions. Visual breaks and details are fine, but all should work together.

18 Now is the time to sand the top sections before they become too thin. Note the small recess on the inner rim opening – I shaped this with a parting tool to help the insert sit better.

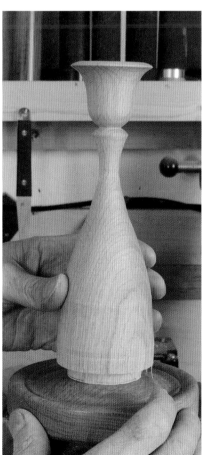

19 I have taken off the work to show how the two parts look at this stage in relation to each other. By placing things together like this, you can more easily see what needs to be removed and adjusted. Be careful when doing this, however; removing is tricky, because it doesn't always go back in the chuck perfectly centered. However, you can use the tailstock to support and re-center the piece. You need this centered properly between centers from here on in.

20 Once between centers with the tenon end nearest the headstock, use a beading and parting tool to reduce the tenon to the size that fits in the hole in the base.

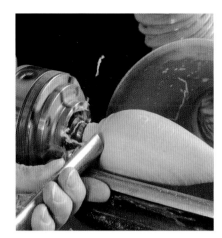

21 Refine the stem section with a spindle roughing gouge. The main bulb of the stem needs to blend in nicely with the lowest upper section and of course flow into the base section without looking too fat. Check the fit regularly as you go by removing the piece and fitting it into the base.

22 With a spindle gouge, refine the shape some more using only small cuts. I call this type of shaping "teasing the shape into being." It is a gentle process, using a combination of sight and touch until you think it is right. This thinner section needs to be strong enough to hold some weight, but thin enough to create an airiness about it.

23 When you think you are close to finishing, take the candlestick off the lathe and check once again.

24 The tenon was too long, so I used a parting tool to remove some waste, leaving a small stub that will be cut off once the piece is removed. Before that, the piece is sanded through the grit grades.

25 Now remove the candlestick from the lathe, apply some glue in the hole (I used medium thickness cyanoacrylate for speed), and insert the stem section before quickly placing the whole assembly between centers. This keeps everything in line and acts as a clamp.

26 Once the glue has dried, use a beading and parting tool to angle the side of the base section and shape the rest of the bead form. Adjust the shape and angle to suit your preferences and sand it. With a parting tool, remove most of the tenon used earlier to hold the base section. Leave enough so that it can withstand the waxing that follows. Sand as much of the underside as you can reach, taking care not to touch the chuck at any time.

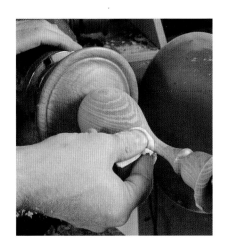

27 Wax all the surfaces you can reach, then remove the candlestick from the lathe, remove the stub, and sand and wax the rest of the base.

TAZZA

> **This modern take** on a classical piece gives you a lot of scope for experimentation. A tazza is basically a supported bowl or platter. Having already created a two-part candlestick (page 130), you have all the skills needed. This project combines both spindle and faceplate turning. The base or pedestal is created with the same techniques used for the candlestick stem. The design can actually be used for a candlestick if you don't stick a platter or bowl on top. The top uses the same techniques as the base of the candlestick and the bowl (page 88), although this is more of a platter. If you cannot find a thick section of wood for the pedestal, consider making your tazza in three parts. Imagine a slightly wider base on the candlestick and a platter on top. This shows where I have been leading you in this book – the interconnectivity of shapes is inescapable, as nothing is really viewed in isolation. I chose to have a color contrast of a deep rich brown in the brown oak platter and the creamy white of the sycamore pedestal. Color contrast is a great way of adding visual interest.

You will need:

- Spindle roughing gouge
- Spindle gouge
- Beading and parting tool
- Thin parting tool
- Skew chisel
- Bowl gouge
- Bead-forming tool
- Scraper
- Scroll chuck
- Screw chuck or faceplate
- Calipers
- Drill chuck with bit
- Drive spur
- Live center
- Abrasives down to 400 grit
- Finish (oil in this case)
- Paper towel
- Adhesive
- Personal protective equipment (PPE): face shield, dust mask, and dust extraction

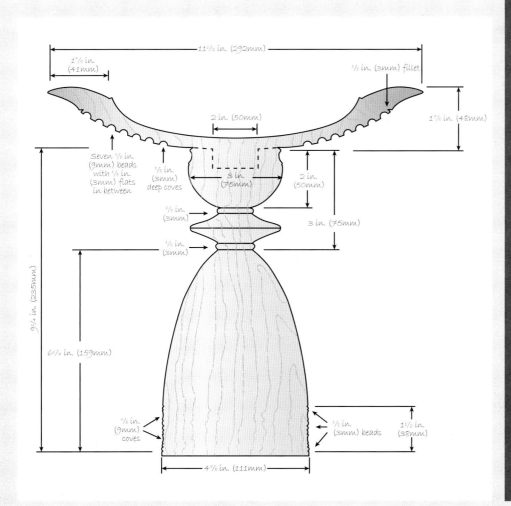

1 Mount the stock for the bowl. I chose a screw held in the chuck. Again, I used the tailstock for support and a pull cut to clean up the surface. If you choose not to use the tailstock, take push cuts instead. Note the two marked circles. One is the bowl's outer rim; the other is where I think the lower bowl form will end and the outer rim detail will start.

2 Define the tenon and use a combination of pull and push cuts to create the rough profile of the lower shape – a gentle upswept curve. Use a parting tool to clean up and define the size of the tenon.

3 Use a push cut to create the sweep on the outermost rim section. This is a sharper-looking transition than you have previously encountered, but it is a classical shape and can work well. Work to a shape you like and incorporate your preferences into designs.

4 Having created the profile, I wanted to add another visual and tactile element and chose to make a series of coves on the lower section of the bowl up to the rim transition. A shaped scraper is the easiest option, although it is does not cut as cleanly as a gouge. When a series of identical shapes are needed, a pre-formed tool helps with uniformity. However, it is important to practice cutting repetitive shapes with gouges in order to develop your skills.

5 I left a flat between each cove. Where they reach the rim area, an incision will separate the lower section nicely. You can use a beading and parting tool or, as I have done, invert a skew chisel and cut with its toe, much the way you would use a point tool scraper. Trail the skew so only the tip of the point touches and scrapes a clean incised line. Don't cut too deep. Sand the surface and the coves.

6 Remove the bowl, mount it in the chuck, and bring up the live center for support. This project calls for a wide rim, which is domed (like the mortar and pestle project on page 94), although it isn't undercut.

7 Remove the waste in sections, working to the live center. Notice the fillet at the innermost section of the rim. This is created with a parting tool and is the point at which the inner section follows the outer lower section. But, because there are deep coves in the outer face, you cannot make the wall too thin.

8 Continue to refine the inner shape, eventually removing the live center so that you can complete the inner curve. Use a scraper if you think it will help.

9 Refine the fillet and sand the surfaces before applying your finish. I like to use oil.

11 Sand any surface just cut and oil this section too. You can see how the beautiful grain pattern of the wood is highlighted once oiled and buffed with paper towel. Remove the piece from the lathe.

10 Use a friction chuck in conjunction with the tailstock to trap and hold the platter in place while you reduce the tenon to the right size. The tenon must fit in the hole that will eventually be cut in the pedestal.

12 Mount the pedestal section between centers. Turn it to a cylinder, clean up one end, then cut a tenon and mount it in the chuck, using the tailstock to center it. Now clean up the tailstock end.

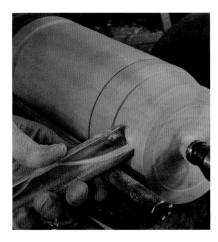

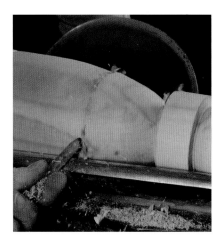

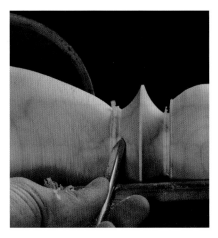

13 Using calipers, mark the outermost diameter required for the cup of the pedestal. Have only the point nearest you in contact with the wood or the other edge will catch and flip the caliper. Mark the main positions of the pedestal detail. I cut them deep enough with a thin parting tool so that when the pedestal is rough-shaped with a spindle roughing gouge, you can still see where everything will be.

14 You can see the cup shape partially formed here. I used a spindle gouge to rough-shape it and add a cove detail at the top, which makes a nice design to lead into the platter. The bullet-shaped body is roughly shaped too, but note the section behind the cup. This will be shaped next. You need to have a gap at either end so you can feed the spindle gouge to the required depth.

15 To create this detail, you work from high to low on either side, as you would to shape a bead. It is two coves coming together, but don't leave a sharp edge at the top, as it would be fragile and could cut someone. A flat or a slight round-over is suitable for this. Getting each side even is tricky – light gentle cuts are the way forward with this.

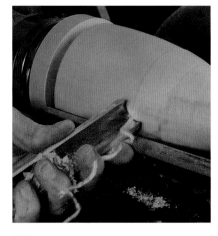

16 On either side, at the same depth, I chose to have a ⅛-in. (3mm) bead, which is a visual separation between the cup and the section just cut, and then the main bullet-shaped body. I used a bead-forming tool because that's easier than cutting small, even beads in such a confined space. If you do not have a bead-forming tool, cut the beads with a combination of a thin parting tool and spindle gouge.

17 Once you have cut the main body, refine its shape with a combination of a spindle roughing gouge and spindle gouge. Note that there is a shallow channel cut near the chuck. The blank was slightly too long for what I wanted, so I marked the bottom of the base and removed the waste section, which will be used for another friction drive on a future project.

18 Now back to the uppermost end of the pedestal. Mark the size of the tenon you cut on the end of the platter, then use a spindle gouge to clean up the end and drill or cut the right-sized hole to match.

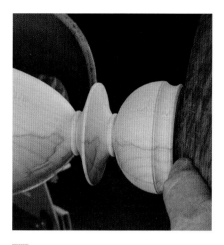

19 Once cut, check for fit, then use a spindle gouge to gently round off the uppermost edge leading into the hole. Note that the lower section of the cove on the cup has an incised line, made with the corner of a parting tool. This creates a nice visual break.

20 When you are happy with the top section, mark the position of the coves and cut them with a spindle gouge. This will give a cleaner cut than using a scraper, but use whatever works for you.

21 At the top and bottom of each cove is a small bead. The forming tool makes light work of this, but you can cut them with other tools if you want to. Go gently with the forming tool so you don't fracture the crowns of the coves.

22 Sand the piece and apply the oil finish. Use a thin parting tool to part almost through at the base. With the lathe stopped, saw off the last bit, clean up the end, and oil it, too. Now all you have to do is glue the platter to the base.

LIDDED BOWL

> **Lidded vessels and** bowls go back to some of the earliest times of human history. Effectively a large form of box, they can be made from spindle- or faceplate-grain wood – this one will be a faceplate-oriented piece. I chose a piece of olive ash for this project, so called because it has beautiful patterning and color that closely resembles European olive wood. I was fortunate enough to have a single hefty piece big enough for me to make the lid and bowl – a piece this size would have been expensive and incredibly hard to find at a hardwood dealer's. If you buy from a dealer, get two pieces, one for the bottom and one for the lid. If you are careful with the wood selection, the grain mismatch will be hard to see.

For an added twist to this bowl I will use a technique to create an undercut foot so that the top inner section of the foot matches the visual line of the outside of the bowl body curve. Beads and coves, used in combination with smooth surfaces, are great decorative features. It is worth experimenting, however; I have had so much fun making lidded forms that in truth if I concentrated on nothing else for the rest of my life I would not get bored.

You will need:

- Bowl gouge
- Beading and parting tool
- Spindle gouge
- Bead-forming tool
- Thin parting tool
- Scraper
- Drill
- Power sanding arbor
- Abrasives down to 320 grit
- Finish of your choice
- Drive spur
- Live center
- Drill bit to fit screw on chuck
- Scroll chuck
- Ruler
- Tissue paper
- Personal protective equipment (PPE): face shield, dust mask, and dust extraction

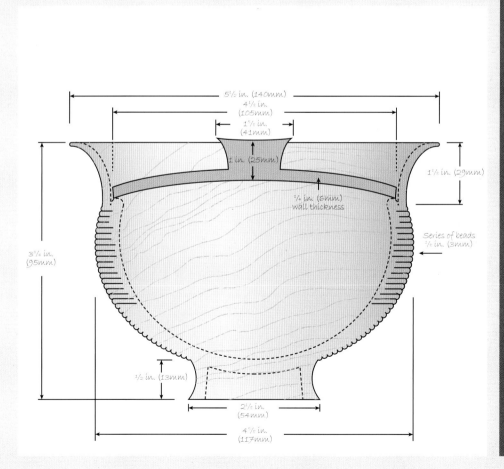

1 As you can see, this piece had some bark on one face that needed to be removed for safety reasons. Although it would have been removed anyway in the course of the project, doing it now will prevent any loose pieces breaking off and causing injury while I am turning the wood.

2 With the bark removed, I marked the centers of the wood. After looking at the piece closely, I opted to use it in faceplate orientation. Since I could not afford to have any screw holes in this piece, I mounted it between centers.

3 I used a bowl gouge to shape the piece. Note that I chose to have the base end nearest the headstock, which meant that I had to cut from the headstock end out. Depending on which hand is your strongest, you may want to mount it the other way so that you cut from the tailstock toward the headstock end, holding it in the chuck to shape the lid.

4 Be sure you cut with the grain to minimize tearout. You can see that this bowl is another ogee, or S-curve, form. It's surprising how versatile this form is and how often it crops up in everyday life. Cut a tenon to fit your chuck. Note the uneven section near the drive spur. This will need to be removed later before fitting the workpiece in the chuck.

5 With the wood still between centers, I applied the bead decoration with a bead-forming tool. Because so many small, tightly aligned beads are needed, this tool helps enormously. But you could use a spindle gouge or parting tool for this, too. Keep the tool at 90° to the face of the work at all times. Note how the top bead forms the boundary of the upswept bottom section of the bowl and the transition with the outward-sweeping rim area.

6 Clean up the top edge, which will become the lid. It will fit on a ledge that will be created on the inner side of the bowl at the same level that the transition from the upsweep of the bottom of the bowl to the outsweep of the rim occurs on the outside of the bowl. Remove the piece from the lathe. I removed the uneven section on the base of the bowl and held the tenon in the chuck. Once you have remounted the piece, partially shape the top of what will be the lid.

7 You can see that I have cut a tenon form on the tailstock end and made a very rough dome cut. The tenon will eventually be turned into the lid handle and the tailstock end will be the top of the lid. Use a thin parting tool to part off the lid from the base section.

8 Make multiple clearance cuts and continually extract the blade to remove the shavings to ensure the blade doesn't jam in the cut. Once done, you have two parts.

9 Use a bowl gouge to shape the bowl about half-way down, making successive cuts and working back to the rim section.

10 Remember that there is a ledge at the transition from the rim to the inner bowl. Once you have shaped the rim, use a scraper to clean it up if needed. Then use a bead-forming tool to detail the ledge I mentioned.

11 Go back to the bowl gouge to create the lower bowl form, staying clear of the bead. There is a slight undercut at the bead to create a nice internal shape.

12 Use a scraper to refine the shape if needed, then sand all the surfaces you can reach before applying the finish of your choice on the inner surfaces. I chose oil.

13 Remove the piece from the lathe and mount the already cut lid form on the tenon. Now measure the overall size of the opening of the ledge.

14 Measure the piece mounted in the chuck to see how much you need to remove. The face shown here will be the underside of the lid. The lid should not be a tight fit. Being turned from one piece, the bowl will move and shrink a little; it will usually go slightly oval, so it is best to allow a very slight clearance gap around the lid to accommodate this movement. A gap of 1/16 in. (1.5mm) all the way around will suffice.

16 Stop the lathe regularly and check for fit. Note that I have not had to remove the work from the lathe to do this.

15 Use a bowl gouge to clean up the face and create a slight hollow to mimic the shape of the dome form cut on the top. The rim of the bowl is flared outward, so you need to angle the rim on this lid to match that shape. If you make the rim square, you may well have the right size where the lid sits on the ledge but, as the rim sweeps away, there will be a huge gap on the top of the lid away from the rim.

17 Once you have the width you need, refine the inner shape and add any additional detail you would like. I chose to cut a couple of beads as a visual link between the lid and the base form. The bead-forming tool was used once again. Sand the freshly cut surfaces and apply your finish.

18 Here you can see the small gap around the lid and the rim. Now mount a waste piece of wood in the chuck and cut a dome on it to fit the inner face of the lid.

19 Cover the shaped waste wood with tissue paper, place the inner face of the lid against this, and bring up the tailstock to hold everything in position. Relocate the live center on the initially marked center still on the tenon. The lid is still a bit thick, so use a bowl gouge to adjust the shape and thickness as required.

20 Having achieved the right shape, I chose to use a spindle gouge to shape the tenon to form the handle for the lid. The overhang is not that great, which minimizes vibration, and the thin cutting edge allows the tool to reach everywhere needed. Be gentle, however, when using it.

21 The shape of the lid is almost akin to a wide, squat top hat. The handle needs to be big enough to hold but not so big that it dominates the lid. After shaping the lid, sand and finish it. Then, using a thin parting tool, remove some of the waste from the top of the handle, cutting almost to the live center. Now remove the lid from the lathe, carve off the little piece of wood left, sand it, and apply your finish.

22 Mount the base on the same waste-wood drive and hold in place with the tailstock. With a low lathe speed, use the thin parting tool to plunge cut into the base to the depth of the lowest bead. You need to make a few cuts to mimic the continuation of the outside curve past the foot. You can cut this quite close, but leave a little stub of wood for the revolving center.

23 Radius off the inner edge of the foot and, once you have only a small stub in the center, remove the piece from the lathe, carve off the stub, and use a small sanding arbor to smooth the inside of the hole. Clean the piece up further before applying the finish.

TIP: The height and width can vary considerably. Experimentation is the key. Stable, dry wood is a must to minimize seasonal movement, although a little will occur due to the release of internal tension in the wood.

QUILTED-ASH VASE

> Open necked or semi-enclosed vases exude elegance. They are not as difficult to turn as people think, although they do look somewhat imposing. This is another spindle-turned project. Remember the scoop you made earlier and the hollowing of the cup section itself? Well, this is an elongated variant of that, so you have already used the techniques that are required; you just need to go deeper than you have so far.

I chose a piece of wood that had a wonderful grain figure – a section of quilted ash. All manner of woods can be used, but the piece I have chosen is not from a branch. The pith could cause problems in this project because the pith is not always stable, which can lead to cracking or distortion. The wood does not have to be figured or a burl – just choose something that catches your eye and is not too tricky to turn. Never put unnecessary hurdles in the way when you are trying things out.

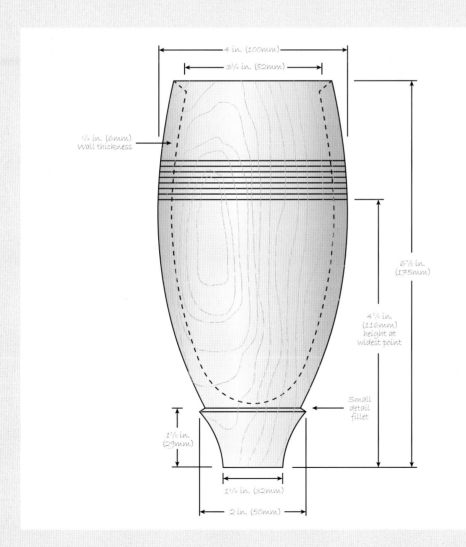

4 in. (100mm)

3¼ in. (82mm)

¼ in. (6mm)
Wall thickness

6⅞ in. (175mm)

4⁵⁄₈ in. (116mm) height at widest point

Small detail fillet

1⅛ in. (29mm)

1¼ in. (32mm)

2 in. (50mm)

You will need:

- Spindle roughing gouge
- Spindle gouge
- Beading and parting tool
- Thin parting tool
- Live center
- Drive spur
- Scroll chuck
- Scraper
- Abrasives down to 400 grit
- Forceps or extension for sanding arbor
- Drill chuck
- 1½-in. (38mm) and ⅞-in. (22mm) Forstner or sawtooth bits
- Oil finish
- Personal protective equipment (PPE): face shield, dust mask, and dust extraction

1 You know the drill by now. With the wood mounted between centers, create a cylinder and cut a tenon for your chuck at the headstock end. Rough-shape the vase, with the base section at the headstock end. Don't make the base too thin yet. Use a beading and parting tool to clean up what will be the open end of the vase near the tailstock.

2 You can see more clearly in this photo how far I got. The widest part of the vase is about one-third of the way down from the top edge. I chose to refine the shape a bit more so I could tell where to hollow to later. Cutting close to the required final external shape at this early stage will help you gauge wall thickness more easily.

3 You can see the shape developing nicely. Again, don't make the base section thin yet; you have to leave enough strength for it to resist the forces of hollowing the inside. A spindle roughing gouge is an ideal tool to do the shaping of these gentle curves. Cut gently downhill with the grain to minimize any chip out. Figured wood might be problematic at times because the interlocking grain can chip.

4 The next stage is to start hollowing out the middle. I chose a large bit to drill down to the widest part; I will use a smaller bit later on to go deeper. You can of course use hollowing techniques with a gouge. You can also speed things up a little by drilling out some waste before using another technique. The choice is yours but, if drilling, remember to retract the cutter regularly to remove the chips so the bit does not jam in the hole.

5 Once drilled to your required depth, refine the opening with a gouge. Use the hollowing techniques featured earlier when making the scoop (page 64). You should always remove the live center or, in this instance, the drill bit, to avoid having your arm or elbow hit the exposed tailstock accessories.

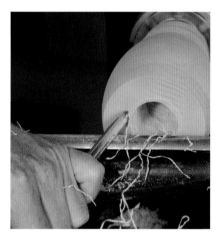

6 Use a spindle gouge to clean up the opening. The face is angled into the work, so technically the cut is against the grain. Note the lower handle angle and the cutting edge peeling off the shavings. This presentation angle is similar to a skew chisel's cutting angle and is a great cut to know.

7 A gouge will make light work of removing waste in the upper section.

8 Use a scraper to clean up the piece further. A tipped tool is very handy for this. I used one with a bullet tip, but any scraping tip of a shape that fits the surface being worked on would be suitable. One advantage of the bullet-shaped tip is that it can also be used for hollowing.

9 Now you need to go deeper. I used a smaller drill bit to remove the waste down to about two-thirds of the depth of the inner section. Remove the shavings regularly by extracting the cutter. Now, refine the side wall and blend the top section in with the next section down. The wall needs to be relatively even.

10 Use the tipped tool to extend the inner hollow. Remember to always cut on or above the centerline of the work and never lower the handle below the level of the tip. It is better to trail the tip below the handle and rotate the blade to create a gentle cut; this minimizes the risk of catching. The deeper you cut, the higher the rest needs to be to ensure the right cutting position.

11 I used a smaller cutter here to go just short of the final required depth, followed by the tipped tools for further hollowing. I measured the overall length of the drill so I knew just how deep to go. Alternatively, measure and apply tape or draw a line on the drill bit at the right depth.

12 You can see here that the vase is almost done. Be warned, however: cutting deeply into a form can be difficult. The deeper you go, the further the tool hangs unsupported over the toolrest. Consequently, the thicker the shaft must be to prevent vibration. This project is, in my opinion, the limit of a ½-in. (13mm) shaft.

13 After refining the shape internally, sand it to a fine finish. I used forceps to hold the abrasive, but other methods can be used too.

14 You can use a sanding arbor, although you may need an extension rod for it. Also consider using a stick with abrasive wrapped on the end. Sand the rim too.

15 Refine the outside with a spindle gouge. Make sure the outside closely follows the shape of the inner hollow. Any refinements need to be small for the main body, but of course you have waste wood in the lower section near the chuck.

16 By now you will have noted that I like to use some form of decorative effect, but only if it helps with the visual and tactile elements. For the base section, I wanted to create the visual effect of the main body of the hollow form floating on a support base. So, once again I used a fillet to create a visual separation of foot section from body without affecting the visual continuation of the curve too much.

17 I also felt the body needed something more, so I decided to make a few grooves – an odd number (I always feel odd numbers are better, maybe because it helps me see a center point). As in previous projects, the corner of a parting tool works well for this. Sand the outside to a fine surface finish.

18 Once you have finished sanding, oil the inside of the hollow and the main body. Wipe off the excess after a few minutes. The forceps came in handy to hold the cloth for wiping up the excess oil.

 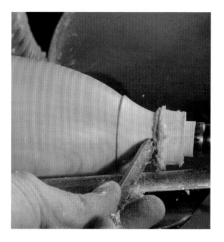 

19 Once it is oiled, remove the work from the chuck, fit a waste-wood section in the chuck, and create a taper to fit the opening of the vase.

20 Place paper towel over the taper and slide on the vase. Bring up the tailstock for support and refine the bottom section of the foot. A spindle gouge will help you refine the outside form, and a parting tool will help undercut and remove some of the waste from the base. Stop short of the live center.

21 Sand the unfinished areas before applying oil. Remove the piece from the lathe, cut off the waste, and sand the rest of the base before oiling it.

SALT OR PEPPER MILL

> **Making mills involves** following a few key steps to ensure that all the relevant parts come together well and is, at least for the internal elements of this design, an exercise in drilling. It is probably true to say that the CrushGrind® shaft mechanism I've chosen affords the most freedom for you to experiment with shape, but fitting the mechanism requires precise measuring, drilling, and turning to get the elements to lock in properly. For this project, it is best to use sawtooth or Forstner bits in a drill chuck. Although more expensive than other tools, you can use the bits over and over. If you do not have one, buy a short-shaft mechanism and use a combination of beading and parting tool and gouge, or one of the hollowing/scraper hybrid tools shown at the beginning of the book, although this is a more complex route. I chose spalted beech for this project, although any hardwood will be suitable.

You will need:

- Spindle roughing gouge
- Spindle gouge
- Beading and parting tool
- Thin parting tool
- Bead-forming tool
- Skew chisel
- Scroll chuck
- Drill chuck
- 1½-in. (38mm) and ⅞-in. (22mm) Forstner or sawtooth bits
- Drive spur
- Live center
- Abrasives
- Paper towel
- Sanding sealer and wax
- 8-in. (200mm) CrushGrind shaft mechanism
- Personal protective equipment (PPE): face shield, dust mask, and dust extraction

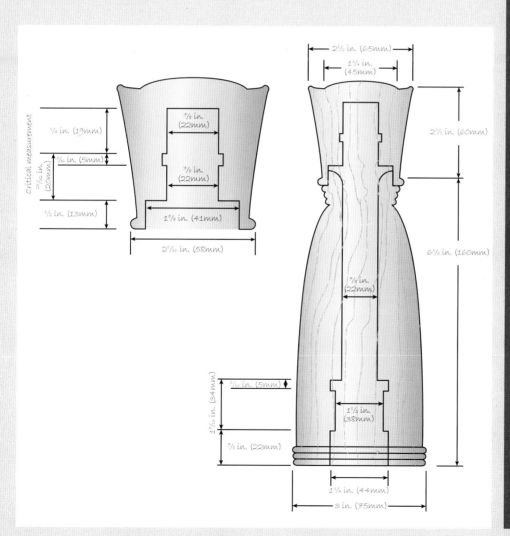

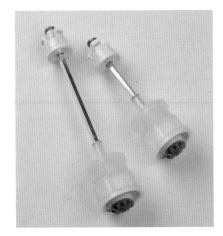

1 Here are two CrushGrind shaft mechanisms of different lengths – other sizes are available. The lower grinding section of the mechanism is self-contained and is bonded to the shaft. The top plastic section – the shaft drive – is fitted into the head of the mill and locks onto the shaft, rotating it when turned.

2 The critical elements need measuring precisely, including the spring-loaded locking lugs. Follow the drawing and you can see what critical measurements need to be used.

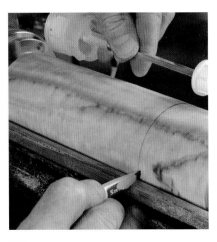

3 Mount a piece of wood between centers and create a cylinder. Use a beading and parting tool to cut a tenon on each end, then mount the cylinder in the chuck and bring up the tailstock. Here, I am marking where the top and the base section will be.

4 Having established the main body and head positions, and ensuring that each part is long enough to house the grind mechanism, use a beading and parting tool to define a tenon. I chose to have the tenon on the main body, but you can have it on the top section if you prefer. Use a thin parting tool to remove the top from the bottom, leaving a little reference point for the tenon in the top.

5 I chose to keep the drilling simple by using a ⅞-in. (22mm) bit for the reservoir to hold the salt or pepper. The lathe should be running at about 200 rpm. The drill is used in a drill chuck. Remember to extract the bit regularly to clear the shavings.

6 Once you have drilled as far as you can go, use a spindle gouge to clean up the shoulder and the outside of the tenon. Then gently radius the inner edge and sand the inside and the tenon. I used forceps to hold the abrasive to sand the hole.

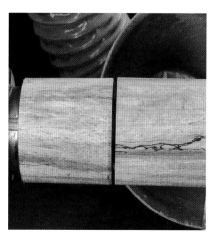

7 Remove the body section from the chuck and fit the top section of the mill in the chuck. You can see here that there is enough wood on the body section to fully house the mechanism and enough on the top section to house the shaft drive. Be sure to check that your own piece is long enough.

8 Use a spindle gouge to hollow out some of the waste for the spindle housing, using the cut featured in the scoop (page 64) and modern candlestick (page 58).

9 Clean up the side walls of the tenon housing with a beading and parting tool, working to just shy of the tenon reference. Check for fit regularly and adjust for depth and fit as required. You can see I need to go a bit deeper here to get the body and top to fit together.

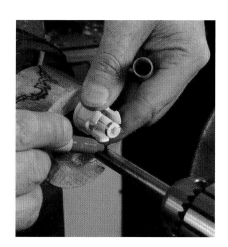

10 Mount the drill in the tailstock and, with the ⅞-in. (22mm) drill used previously, drill ⅞ in. (22mm) deep to house the shaft drive. The wider section will sit proud on the face.

11 Here, you can see the shaft-drive lugs. A swivel-tip scraper with a suitable tip or tip you have shaped yourself is ideal for being able to create the recess needed to lock the shaft-drive lugs in place.

12 This tip will create an angled recess. You can have the tip at 90° and cut a square recess if you prefer. Then go back with the ⅞-in. (22mm) drill and bore an additional ⅞ in. (22mm) deep.

13 Fit the shaft drive in the top and then slide the metal shaft in place. Bring up the bottom section of the mill, then place the shoulders together and check everything. You can see that the mill head will sit in the main body bottom nicely when everything is cleaned up.

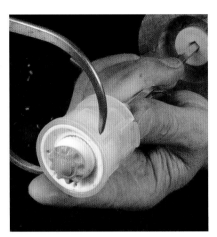

14 I checked that the 1½-in. (38mm) bit is what is needed for the body of the grinding mechanism. Note the small shoulder near the end.

15 Remove the mill top from the lathe and mount the base section, holding it on the mating tenon already cut. Tighten the chuck enough to stop the workpiece from spinning while you bore it out. The jaws I used do not mark the tenon, although dovetail jaws might. Off the lathe, sand away any light marks, then measure and mark the position of the recess and top of the grinding mechanism.

16 The 1½-in. (38mm) bit is used to bore the hole for the mill body, which is 1⁵⁄₁₆in (34mm) long, plus whatever you leave in depth for a recess – about 2⅛ in. (54mm) in total depth. This is followed by the ⅞-in. (22mm) bit to meet up with the hole drilled from the top.

17 Now sand the two holes and cut the recess for the lugs.

18 Remove the body from the chuck and mount some waste wood in the chuck (endgrain orientation is needed). Cut a tenon that fits snugly in the large holes. It needs to be a tight fit.

19 Mount the body onto the tenon. You can see that it supports the body nicely.

20 Put tissue paper over the mating tenon, pop on the lid, and bring up the tailstock.

21 Now the fun part: shaping the body. The design is entirely up to you. I love architecture and towers, so I wanted something akin to that. I shaped the main body like the tazza body section (page 142) and had the top sweep up and out from the joint. I used a spindle roughing gouge for this.

22 I also wanted to include a decorative effect, and since we have been using beads (one of the most versatile decorative elements around), I placed a series of them at the central joint and at the top outer edge of the lid. A bead-forming tool is ideal for this. I then used a thin parting tool to roll the beads.

23 The base end also has some beads, three in this case. I much prefer odd numbers for beads, grooves, and similar decoration – it just seems to look better than even numbers.

24 Use a beading and parting tool to remove the tenon on the top of the lid. Next, use a spindle gouge to refine the outer edge before rough-shaping the dome on the end, leaving clear a bit of wood under the live center.

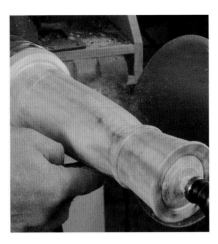

25 Sand the complete outside shape.

26 Check that you have not removed too much from the end of the lid.

27 I chose to refine the dome further with a spindle gouge, using a shear cut. I then removed all the pieces from the lathe, carved off the stub near the live center, and sanded the dome fully.

28 I made a mistake when it came to fitting the mechanism in the base. I forgot to cut a 1¾-in.-wide (45mm) recess to a depth of ¾ in. (19mm) for the shoulder of the grinding head. So, I re-mounted the base section, holding it in the mating tenon. Of course, you could use a jam chuck for this.

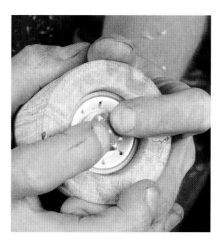

29 Using very light cuts to avoid putting much pressure on the chuck, I cut the recess to the right depth. Of course, this should have been done at stage 18. Still, I always learn something from my mistakes.

30 When I fitted the mechanism, it clicked in place within the recess nicely because the wood was quite soft. However, you are likely to have to make a jig to fit over the mechanism so you can tap it in place.

31 Now you can fit the mill top and base section together. Apply sanding sealer to the piece – you can brush it on or use an aerosol. Then, when the sealed surface has fully dried, denib the surface with oil or wax. I used wax, applied with paper towel.

TIP: This is the one project in this book that requires more than the basic set of tools. You must also be technically very precise to get this project right.

SPINNING TOP

> **Fun to make,** spinning tops are also a good test of your skills. They take me back to my days in primary school, before the age of computers and the like, where friends and I used to have competitions to see whose top would spin the longest. Or, we would mark a circle and spin the tops and see whose knocked the other one out of the "ring" or caused the opponent's top to stop. Fun indeed!

For this spindle-turned project, I chose a hard, close-grained exotic wood called purpleheart. I wanted something dense, easy to work, durable, and able to hold fine detail. The ability of the wood to hold fine detail is vital. The spinning point needs to remain sharp, and the thin stem must be strong and resilient. Maple is a good low-cost option. Once the wood is mounted in the chuck, everything is done from this one chucking mount. The sequence of cuts is very important for success. Start from the underneath point, working back to the stem. The center of gravity needs to be low so the piece will spin properly. Too high and it won't work very well if at all.

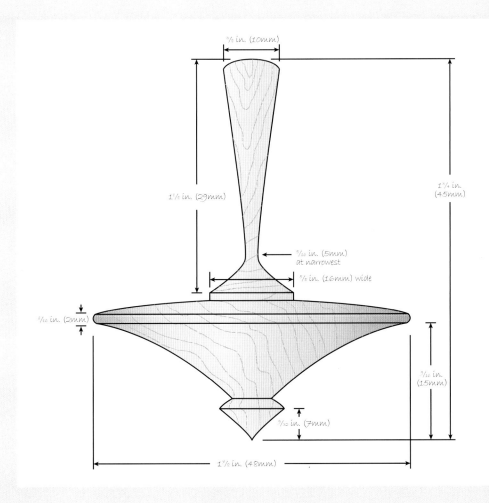

⅜ in. (10mm)

1⅛ in. (29mm)

1¾ in. (45mm)

³⁄₁₆ in. (5mm) at narrowest

⅝ in. (16mm) wide

¹⁄₁₆ in. (2mm)

⁹⁄₁₆ in. (15mm)

⁹⁄₃₂ in. (7mm)

1⅞ in. (48mm)

You will need:

- Spindle roughing gouge
- Spindle gouge
- Skew chisel
- Beading and parting tool
- Thin parting tool
- Scroll chuck
- Abrasives down to 400 grit
- Paste wax finish
- Personal protective equipment (PPE): face shield, dust mask, and dust extraction

2 After you make the initial shaping cuts, use fine cuts to refine the surface and create a delicate point on which to spin the top. You can add a nice visual detail by creating a small angled fillet just back from the point, giving the appearance that the main spinning body "floats" on the tip section. It is nothing other than visual, but you must not have the body too tall overall – the top's center of gravity will be too high and it will not spin properly.

1 I had a square offcut of purpleheart, which I mounted into the chuck jaws. If you do not have something similar, you can mount the wood between centers, create a cylinder, and mount it in the chuck. I used a spindle roughing gouge to create the parallel cylinder section on the square and a spindle gouge to create the curve on the lower section.

3 Use a skew chisel to refine the fillet detail.

4 Once you have created this detail, sand the flared-out body section and the tip section, including the point of the tip. Some round it off – there is a debate as to whether a rounded or sharp point is better. I will let you decide which you prefer. Dense wood can be sanded to very fine grit grades. I stopped at 400 grit.

5 Apply the paste wax with your finger and then buff it with paper towel.

6 Use a beading and parting tool to create a chamfer at the widest point of the spinning body.

8 Take a spindle gouge and refine the top of the body. Being ambidextrous helps here. The cut ideally suits a left-handed person; right-handers need to tuck their bodies up against the lathe to get the angle of attack for the cut.

7 Use the same tool to part a ⅜-in.-wide (10mm) groove behind the spinning body. Leave the depth of the body slightly thicker than needed at this stage and leave about 1 in. (25mm) for the stem.

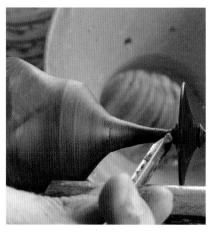

10 I created a small shoulder detail on the top to help with a visual transition from step to body. Use a thin parting tool to create the shoulder and a spindle gouge for the cuts down from this to the stem section. Before you go too slim, sand the top of the body.

9 Once you have the basic shape of the body top, use a spindle gouge to cut away some of the waste wood where the stem will be, gradually creating that nice curve.

12 Now for the tricky part. You need to thin down the stem, working back in small sections at a time. You already have the lowest part behind the body. Cut downward to this lowest part, gradually creating the stem form you like.

11 Apply paste wax and buff it carefully, using finger support if needed.

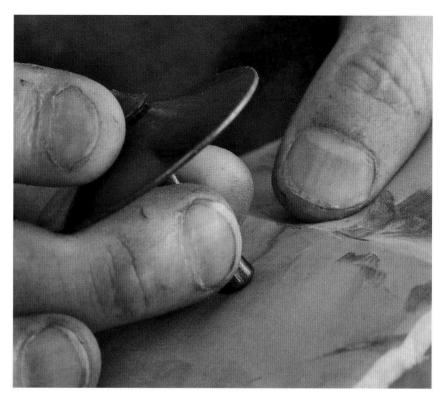

13 Once the stem is done, you need to sand it and then wax it before using a skew chisel to remove the stem from the waste section of wood. Again, I supported the spinning top while the cuts were made. A few cuts will be needed to do this as cleanly as possible. All body parts and clothing should be out of the way of any spinning parts.

14 Sand and finish the top of the stem.

FINIAL BOX

> **This box can be described** as an egg with a finial, with the egg supported
by a pedestal. This spindle-turned project integrates the skills you have used in
the spinning top (page 166) and the simple box (page 82). The way the shapes
are integrated is more complex, but there is nothing here that you have not done
already. You just need a little finer tool control. I chose a branch of laburnum for
this project. I love the color contrast of the heartwood with the sapwood. Although
the heartwood is a greenish brown when freshly cut, it changes color to a rich
chocolate with a pronounced grain pattern, which is in stark contrast to the creamy
sapwood. Because there is a delicate finial on this project, you need a reasonably
dense hardwood that will hold fine detail. The finial must also be thick enough to
withstand someone using it to pick up the piece.

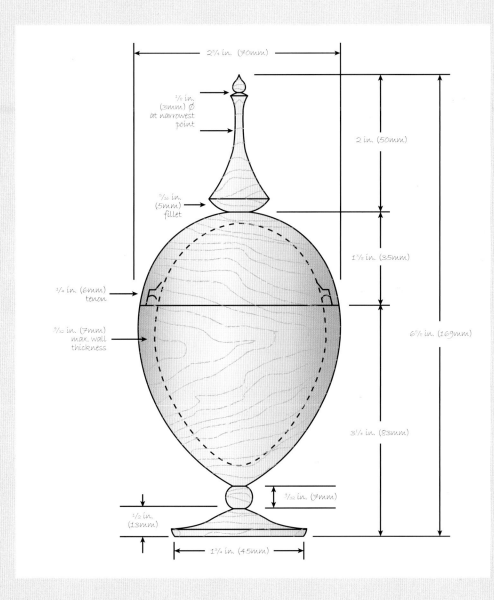

2¾ in. (70mm)

⅛ in.
(3mm) Ø
at narrowest
point

2 in. (50mm)

³⁄₁₆ in.
(5mm)
fillet

1⅜ in. (35mm)

¼ in. (6mm)
tenon

6⅝ in. (169mm)

⁹⁄₃₂ in. (7mm)
max. wall
thickness

3¼ in. (83mm)

⁹⁄₃₂ in. (7mm)

½ in.
(13mm)

1¾ in. (45mm)

You will need:

- Spindle roughing gouge
- Spindle gouge
- Beading and parting tool
- Thin parting tool
- Scraper with round or French-curve cutting edge
- Scroll chuck
- Skew chisel
- Live center
- Drive spur
- Duct tape
- Abrasives down to 400 grit
- Finish of your choice
- Personal protective equipment (PPE): face shield, dust mask, and dust extraction

1 Mount the wood between centers, create a cylinder, and cut a tenon at one end. Stop the lathe, mount the wood in the chuck, and bring up the tailstock for support. Cut a tenon at the tailstock end.

2 Use a spindle roughing gouge to cut all the major body shapes, leaving them oversized at this stage. The body shape will have a tenon, so it needs to be elongated to account for this.

3 Use a beading and parting tool to shape this tenon, which is slightly tapered. What you can see here is the top of the box with the finial at the end nearest the tailstock. But you need to cut the body of the box before shaping the finial, hence its current shape. Use a beading and parting tool to mark where the tenon will be.

4 Use a spindle gouge to further shape the lower section of the box. Try to visualize how the two parts come together and shape it accordingly, so the shape is correct when the two parts are joined.

5 Use a thin parting tool to separate the base from the lid. In this instance, the tenon is left on the base.

6 I left a marker on the lid to show the width of the tenon cut. You can work to this or a smaller wall, but not bigger – you will not have enough thickness to adjust the outer shape later on.

TIP: Finials are fun to make. They look interesting and add drama to a piece. Be aware, though, that they are often used as the holding point to lift a lid. This makes them prone to breaking, especially if they are very thin or the lid is tight-fitting.

7 Using a spindle gouge, employ the endgrain hollowing technique learned previously (page 54).

8 Follow this by using a scraper or moving directly to abrasive, as required. The inner-edge tenon will need to be adjusted for height and width later on, so leave it alone for the moment. Remove this piece from the lathe.

9 Fit the lid section in the chuck on the tenon already cut. Hollow out the body with a spindle gouge.

10 You need to cut a recess, or shoulder, for the tenon to fit into and lock onto. This means doing this with a parting tool of some sort. Don't go too deep because you have an arced surface on the outer face of the lid, which is not too thick at this point.

11 Check the base section for fit regularly, making sure the lathe is off. Stop adjusting the recess when it is just wide enough to allow the topmost part of the tenon to enter the recess.

12 Slightly undercut what will be the meeting face of the box to its lower partner. Sand the inside section and apply your finish. Once done, remove this part from the lathe.

TIP: As you are no doubt aware, the visual balance of any work is paramount. The body and lid should be about two-thirds to one-third ratio. The foot and the finial should be similar sizes. Experiment to find out what you think works best.

13 Refit the base section and shorten the tenon so that it fits in the recess without hindrance. Radius the inner edge – the last thing you want is a sharp edge where fingers may go.

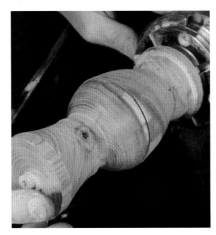

14 Slightly adjust the outer face of the tenon and chamfer the meeting shoulder so that it sits squarely on the outer section of its mating piece. Check the lid for fit.

15 Once you are happy with the fit, sand and apply a finish to the inside.

16 As with the previous box project, place paper towel over the box opening and fit the lid onto that. You want a firm fit, but not one so tight it breaks the walls of the box. Once fitted, bring up the tailstock for support and use a spindle gouge to refine the body shape of the box.

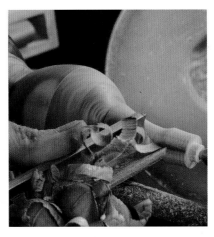

17 Use a spindle roughing gouge to remove the waste section of what will become the finial.

18 You can see the white line of the paper towel in the tenon. A spindle gouge is used to create the lower section of the finial.

TIP: To minimize the risk of making mistakes, take slow, controlled cuts. It is also important to stop regularly and check on your progress.

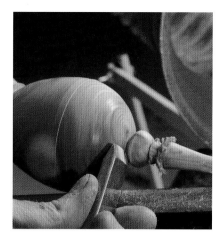

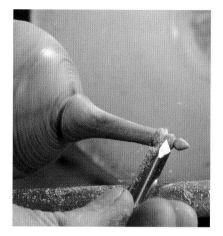

19 It looks like it is going to be a bead, but it isn't – I have simply rounded the lower part near the box body. Use a skew chisel to get into the lower section cleanly. Don't make this too thin; you still need to cut the finial.

20 Partially shape the finial body with a spindle gouge, leaving everything oversized at the moment, and then shape the very end. Note that the tailstock has been removed.

21 The tip is a minaret-type form. Create a shoulder at its base, which is the top of the main curved body of the finial. Delicately work from the tip down to the lowest section of the curve.

22 I noticed some "give" on the tenon section when cutting. I did not wish to use more tissue paper in the joints, so I decided to wrap duct tape around the outer face of the joint to provide extra support while shaping the finial. Once you have reached the lowest section you can work the thicker section, to blend down to the lowest.

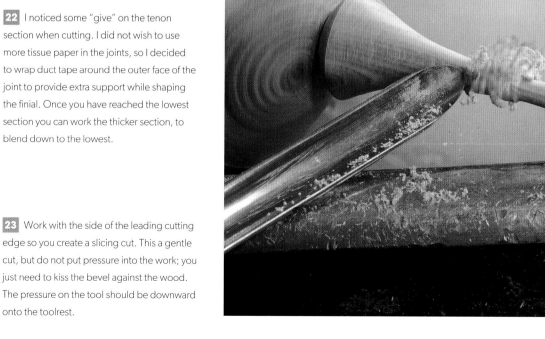

23 Work with the side of the leading cutting edge so you create a slicing cut. This a gentle cut, but do not put pressure into the work; you just need to kiss the bevel against the wood. The pressure on the tool should be downward onto the toolrest.

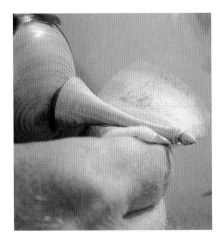

24 When you are satisfied with the shape, sand the finial, using gentle pressure.

25 You can now remove the tape from the main body and refine the lower body section of the box with a spindle gouge. Make sure that everything is secure before starting up the lathe, and err toward slower speeds at this stage. You need the lid in place to get the body shape right but you don't want the lid to fly off.

26 Now you can sand the main body and apply your finish.

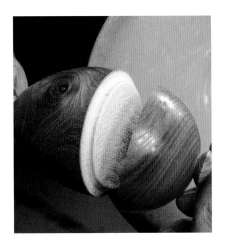

27 Remove the lid, because you no longer need it in place.

28 Remove the base section and fit a piece of waste wood in the chuck that is large enough that you can cut a taper to accommodate the inner hollow. Place paper towel over it before you fit on the box bottom. Once that is done, bring up the live center and lock it in place. Start to refine the base with a spindle gouge.

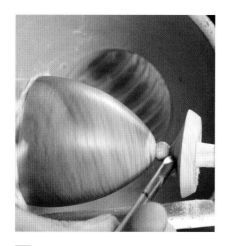

29 Remove some waste so you can better shape the bead that separates the bottom of the box from the foot section. You should have enough access only to use either a spindle gouge or a parting tool for this.

30 Shape the edge of the foot and reduce the tenon down to a little stub.

31 Sand and apply your finish. Remove the box and clean up the bottom.

TIP: While I chose laburnum for this project, you have many other options. Hardwoods give you strength, but yew (a softwood) would also work well. Do be careful of branches or logs, though. The pith is generally prone to being unsound; if the pith line runs along or slightly off-center but through the finial or head, it weakens the piece and may lead to breakage.

TREE ORNAMENT

> **Multicolored baubles of every** conceivable shape and size are widely available
to buy, but it is a great idea to try making Christmas tree decorations yourself. This
ornament is a wonderful way of using all the skills you have learned so far in this
book in a different kind of project. If you use low-density softwoods, you can make
thin icicles in one piece without them being too heavy. This ornament is a form
made in three parts. I am using quilted maple for the body – a small hollow form –
contrasting with African blackwood for the top and the drop finial. Choose what
woods you like and play around. There are so many shapes to go for.

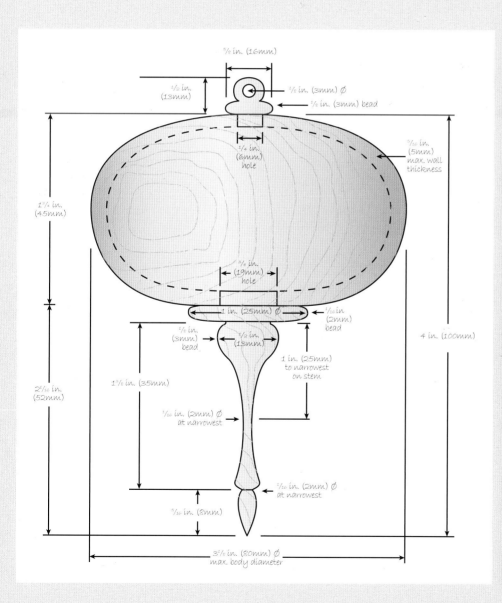

You will need:

- Spindle roughing gouge
- Spindle gouge
- Beading and parting tool
- Thin parting tool
- Scraper with round or French-curve cutting edge
- Scroll chuck
- Calipers
- Live center
- Drive spur
- Duct tape
- Abrasives down to 400 grit
- Finish of your choice
- Line or wire to suspend ornament
- Drill with drill bit to suit line or wire used to suspend ornament
- Personal protective equipment (PPE): face shield, dust mask, and dust extraction

1 Let's start with the body. Mount the blank between centers and create a cylinder. Cut a tenon at one end.

2 Use a spindle gouge to create the body shape you want. I chose a squat bead form.

3 You can drill or use a spindle gouge to create a hole through the piece before opening up the hole near the tailstock to accommodate the bottom drop finial. This is the hole you will be hollowing through. By using a gouge, you can use the hollowing technique shown in the simple box project (page 82). You will not, however, be able to reach fully under the rim. Also, do not go too deep or the piece will not be stable for hollowing under the rim.

4 You can effectively hollow by sweeping the gouge from the center out in a fan shape that, once completed, is all you can do with the gouge. The downside of working through a small hole is you have to stop and clear out the shavings regularly.

5 To achieve the shape required for this project, use either a shaped scraper, a scraper, or cutting tool that allows you to reach around the shoulder. A swan-necked, articulated or swivel-tip scraper will do this. If you do not have one, just change the body shape so you can reach all the areas with a gouge or standard straight scraper. Whatever you use, adjust the opening shape to make sure you can move the tools to where you need to get to without hitting the side walls.

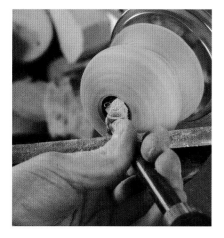

6 The tool should be supported on the toolrest by the main shank, not any other part. Angle the cutter to reach where you need to go and make gentle cuts above the centerline of the form – never below it.

7 Once you have run the cutter around the inside and produced an even wall thickness, use a beading and parting tool to reduce the waste on the chuck-side of the form.

8 Sand and apply the finish of your choice. Again, I used oil.

9 Part off the work. No part of me is near the chuck, so I am clear to hold the work gently while I part it off. Remember, there is a hole running through the piece.

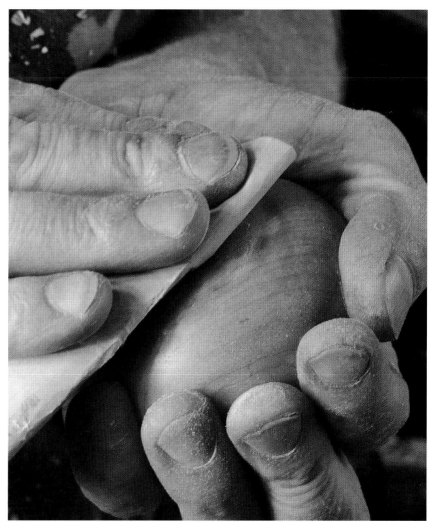

TIP: The body shape is not critical. Experiment and adapt it to the shape of wood you have. It can be wide and squat or tall and thin. When finished, it does need to be very light weight so that the tree branches can support it without bending.

10 Once parted off, clean up the upper end of the piece and apply your choice of finish.

11 The lower finial is a section of a piece of African blackwood from what is sold as a clarinet bell blank. One of these quadrants will do four complete projects like this for me.

12 The thickest end can be gripped in the central section of your chuck jaws. The live center can be brought up to support the piece while you create the taper. African blackwood takes excellent details but is dusty to use.

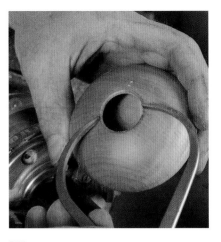

13 Measure the opening of the widest hole.

14 Measure the overall length of the finial required, then use a beading and parting tool to cut the tenon to the proper diameter to suit the length previously measured. This establishes the mating joint and the overall length of the finial. Use a spindle gouge to start shaping the finial.

15 Use a spindle gouge to shape a partial bead on the part nearest the tenon. Note how there is a wider section at the pointed side of that tenon. This allows the tenon to fit in the hole and provides a shoulder to cover the hole. It's also a nice detail. Shape the tip end of this bead and then start to refine the finial shape, working from the very tip back to the bead.

16 Blackwood cuts cleanly if you use a shearing or peeling cut. As with previous finials, create the main curve of the finial slowly and carefully. The thinnest part is about one-third of the way down from the top. Near the shoulder, the stem is rolled over to create a nice intersection with the beaded shoulder area.

17 Once shaped, sand it.

18 Apply your finish. Oil and paste wax was used in this case. As before, apply only gentle pressure, then buff with paper towel.

19 Part off the piece through the tenon cut. You need to leave enough on the finial side to equal the wall thickness of the hollow form so it has as much glue area as possible to bond properly.

20 Now try it for fit. You can see here how it should fit in position nicely. Check that the bead detail and shoulder work well visually.

21 Flip the hollow form over and measure the hole created when you pushed the drill or gouge into the wood.

22 Create another tenon on the blackwood held in the chuck, making it slightly bigger than the hole opening. Use a spindle gouge to cut a little ball on its front end.

23 Drill a small hole horizontally in the center of the ball. The hole only needs to be big enough for some fishing line or a ribbon to be passed through it.

24 Once drilled, refine the shape of the ball.

25 Turn a bead form on the shoulder of the tenon at the base of the ball. A bead-forming tool works well for this, but a gouge or parting tool would also work.

26 Create a tenon sized to fit in the hole. You can see how calipers and a thin parting tool work well for this. The tenon needs to be overlong so you can part off the right length. Undercut the topmost shoulder of the beaded part so it sits flush against the hollow form. Do not part it off yet.

27 Sand the piece carefully and apply your finish. Buff it with paper towel, then part it off.

28 Now glue the lower finial and upper button in place.

TIP: The ornament can be suspended on the tree by fishing line, wire, or specially shaped clips. A personalized tree ornament makes a beautiful gift.

SUPPLIERS

I have given contact details for suppliers and manufacturers whose products I have used in this book. There are many others that I do not have space to mention; you will find them in local directories and woodworking magazines.

UNITED STATES

Craft Supplies USA
1287 E. 1120 S.
Provo, UT 84608
Tel: 1-800-551-8876
www.woodturnerscatalog.com

Easy Wood Tools
1365 Cahill Drive
Lexington, KY 40504
Tel: 1-866-963-0294
www.easywoodtools.com

Highland Woodworking
1045 N. Highland Avenue N.E.
Atlanta, GA 30306
Tel: 1-800-241-6748
www.highlandwoodworking.com

Packard Woodworks Inc.
215 S. Trade Street
Tryon, NC 28782
Tel: 1 828 859 6762
Toll-free (USA and Canada only):
1-800-683-8876
www.packardwoodworks.com

Rockler
4365 Willow Drive
Medina, MN 55340
Tel: 1-800-279-4441
www.rockler.com

Thompson Lathe Tools
Doug Thompson
5479 Columbia Road
N. Olmsted, OH 44070
Tel: 1-440-241-6360
www.thompsonlathetools.com

Woodcraft Supply
P.O. Box 1686
Parkersburg, WV 26102-1686
Tel: 1 304 422 5412
Toll-free (USA and Canada only):
1-800-225-1153
www.woodcraft.com

UK

Ashley Iles (Edge Tools) Ltd.
East Kirkby
Spilsby
Lincs PE23 4DD
Tel: +44 (0)1790 763372
www.ashleyiles.co.uk

Axminster Tools & Machinery
Unit 10
Weycroft Avenue
Axminster
Devon EX13 5PH
Tel: +44 (0)3332 406406
www.axminster.co.uk

Behlen Ltd.
Unit 13
Peffermill Parc
25 King's Haugh
Edinburgh
EH16 5UY (by appointment only)
Tel: +44 (0)1316 616812
Toll-free (USA/Canada only): 1-866-785-7781
(non-European enquiries only)
www.behlen.co.uk

Chestnut Products
PO Box 536
Ipswich
IP4 5WN
Tel: +44 (0)1473 425878
www.chestnutproducts.co.uk

Crown Hand Tools Ltd.
332–334 Coleford Road
Damall
Sheffield S9 5PH
Tel: +44 (0)1142 612300
www.crownhandtools.ltd.uk

General Finishes UK
Unit 13
Peffermill Parc
25 King's Haugh
Edinburgh EH16 5UY
(by appointment only)
Tel: +44 (0)1316 615553
www.generalfinishes.co.uk

Hamlet Craft Tools
The Forge
Peacock Estate
Livesey Street
Sheffield S6 2BL
Tel: +44 (0)1142 321338
www.hamletcrafttools.co.uk

Henry Taylor Tools Ltd.
The Forge
Peacock Estate
Livesey Street
Sheffield S6 2BL
Tel: +44 (0)1142 340282 / 321338
www.henrytaylortools.co.uk

Liberon Waxes Ltd.
Mountfield Industrial Estate
Learoyd Road
New Romney
Kent TN28 8XU
Tel: +44 (0)1797 367555
www.liberon.co.uk

Mylands
John Myland Ltd.
26–34 Rothschild Street
London SE27 0HQ
Tel: +44 (0)208 6709161
www.mylands.co.uk

Peter Child
The Old Hyde
Little Yeldham Road
Little Yeldham
Nr Halstead
Essex CO9 4QT
Tel: +44 (0)1787 237291
www.peterchild.co.uk

Record Power Ltd.

Centenary House

11 Midland Way

Barlborough Links

Chesterfield

Derbyshire S43 4XA

Tel: +44 (0)1246 571 020

www.recordpower.co.uk

Robert Sorby

Athol Road

Sheffield S8 0PA

Tel: +44 (0)1142 250700

www.robert-sorby.co.uk

Stiles & Bates

Upper Farm

Church Hill

Sutton

Dover

Kent CT15 5DF

Tel: +44 (0)1304 366360

www.stilesandbates.co.uk

The ToolPost

Unit 7, Hawksworth

Southmead Industrial Park

Didcot

Oxfordshire OX11 7HR

Tel: +44 (0)1235 511101

www.toolpost.co.uk

Turners Retreat

The Woodworkers Source

Faraday Close

Harworth

Notts DN11 8NE

Tel: +44 (0)1302 744344

www.turners-retreat.co.uk

Yandle & Sons Ltd.

Hurst Works

Martock

Somerset TA12 6JU

Tel: +44 (0)1935 822207

www.yandles.co.uk

AUSTRALIA, NEW ZEALAND

Vicmarc Machinery

Teknatool

52 Grice Street

Clontarf

Queensland 4019

Tel: +61 (0)7 3284 3103

www.vicmarc.com

CANADA

Oneway Manufacturing

Unit 1, 291 Griffith Road

Stratford

Ontario N5A 6S4

Tel: 1-519-271-7611

Toll-free (USA and Canada only):

1-800-565-7288

www.oneway.ca

Woodchucker's Supplies

Units 4 & 5

50 Venture Drive

Toronto

Ontario M1B 3L6

Toll-free (USA and Canada only):

1-800-551-0192

www.woodchuckers.com

ACKNOWLEDGMENTS

There are many aspects, including the help of others, that need to come together in order to make a book. I would like to give special thanks to the following people for their kind help and support.

Walter Hall, Mark Sanger, and Chris West for reading the book and making sure I hadn't missed anything and that my comments made sense.

Wendy McAngus for her patience as the book editor.

I would also like to thank the following companies for their assistance.

Ashley Iles (Edge Tools) Ltd., www.ashleyiles.co.uk

Axminster Tools & Machinery, www.axminster.co.uk

Crown Hand Tools, www.crownhandtools.ltd.uk

Henry Taylor Tools Ltd., www.henrytaylortools.co.uk

Record Power, www.recordpower.co.uk

Robert Sorby, www.robert-sorby.co.uk

The ToolPost, www.toolpost.co.uk

Turners Retreat, www.turners-retreat.co.uk

ABOUT THE AUTHOR

Mark Baker has always been fascinated by wood. His father was a carpenter and joiner and, on leaving school, Mark served a five-year apprenticeship working for a local building firm, which included restoration work. Mark has also helped set up an industrial workshop for autistic adults, and he has worked for some of the major manufacturers of woodturning tools in the UK. He is now the editor of *Woodturning* magazine and the group editor of all GMC Publications woodworking magazines. Previous books include *Woodturning Projects: A Workshop Guide to Shapes*, *Wood for Woodturners*, and *Wood Turning: A Craftman's Guide*, all published by GMC Publications.

CONVERSION TABLE

2mm (5/64 in.)	60mm (2⅜ in.)	210mm (8¼ in.)	840mm (33 in.)
3mm (⅛ in.)	63mm (2½ in.)	215mm (8½ in.)	865mm (34 in.)
4mm (5/32 in.)	65mm (2⅝ in.)	220mm (8¾ in.)	890mm (35 in.)
6mm (¼ in.)	70mm (2¾ in.)	230mm (9 in.)	915mm (36 in.)
7mm (9/32 in.)	75mm (3 in.)	235mm (9 ¼in.)	940mm (37 in.)
8mm (5/16 in.)	80mm (3⅛ in.)	240mm (9½ in.)	965mm (38 in.)
9mm (11/32 in.)	85mm (3¼ in.)	250mm (9¾ in.)	990mm (39 in.)
10mm (⅜ in.)	90mm (3½ in.)	255mm (10 in.)	1015mm (40 in.)
11mm (7/16 in.)	93mm (3⅔ in.)	257mm (10⅛ in.)	1040mm (41 in.)
12mm (½ in.)	95mm (3¾ in.)	280mm (11 in.)	1065mm (42 in.)
13mm (½ in.)	100mm (4 in.)	305mm (12 in.)	1090mm (43 in.)
14mm (9/16 in.)	105mm (4⅛ in.)	330mm (13 in.)	1120mm (44 in.)
15mm (9/16 in.)	110mm (4¼–4⅜ in.)	355mm (14 in.)	1145mm (45 in.)
16mm (⅝ in.)	115mm (4½ in.)	380mm (15 in.)	1170mm (46 in.)
17mm (11/16 in.)	120mm (4¾ in.)	405mm (16 in.)	1195mm (47 in.)
18mm (23/32 in.)	125mm (5 in.)	430mm (17 in.)	1220mm (48 in.)
19mm (¾ in.)	130mm (5⅛ in.)	460mm (18 in.)	1245mm (49 in.)
20mm (¾ in.)	135mm (5¼ in.)	485mm (19 in.)	1270mm (50 in.)
21mm (13/16 in.)	140mm (5½ in.)	510mm (20 in.)	1295mm (51 in.)
22mm (⅞ in.)	145mm (5¾ in.)	535mm (21 in.)	1320mm (52 in.)
23mm (29/32 in.)	150mm (6 in.)	560mm (22 in.)	1345mm (53 in.)
24mm (15/16 in.)	155mm (6⅛ in.)	585mm (23 in.)	1370mm (54 in.)
25mm (1 in.)	160mm (6¼ in.)	610mm (24 in.)	1395mm (55 in.)
30mm (1⅛ in.)	165mm (6½ in.)	635mm (25 in.)	1420mm (56 in.)
32mm (1¼ in.)	170mm (6¾ in.)	660mm (26 in.)	1450mm (57 in.)
35mm (1⅜ in.)	178mm (6⅞ in.)	685mm (27 in.)	1475mm (58 in.)
38mm (1½ in.)	180mm (7 in.)	710mm (28 in.)	1500mm (59 in.)
40mm (1⅝ in.)	185mm (7¼ in.)	735mm (29 in.)	1525mm (60 in.)
45mm (1¾ in.)	190mm (7½ in.)	760mm (30 in.)	
50mm (2 in.)	195mm (7¾ in.)	785mm (31 in.)	
55mm (2⅛–2¼ in.)	200mm (8 in.)	815mm (32 in.)	

INDEX

To order a book or to request a catalog, contact:

The Taunton Press, Inc.

63 South Main Street, P.O. Box 5506, Newtown, CT 06470-5506

Tel: (800) 888-8286

www.taunton.com